The Strengths W

Great performers play to their strengths – be it in music, sport or working life. At the same time, they find ways to compensate for their weaknesses. Over the past six years I have tried to follow this philosophy when leading teams and organisations. Perhaps the hardest part is helping people to find and use their real talents – the space where they can do really great work. Mike's book provides many tools for making this happen and I have seen the benefits – both for individuals and organisations. I strongly recommend it to anyone who wants to find and build on people's strengths.

Paul Thomalla, VP EMEA, Stratus Technologies

Mike Pegg is the great encourager, responsible for helping thousands of people to release their inner creativity. The many personal stories woven into the text are truly inspiring, as well as being instructional. The book applies to people in jobs, self employment or unpaid work. Mike says, "everybody has something special to give to the world"; this book will help you to discover just what that is. It will help you to build on your strengths and find your vocation.

Barrie Hopson, Founder, Lifeskills International

I've known Mike Pegg for years. He's a fantastic encourager and his latest book, *The Strengths Way*, is filled with inspiring real-life stories and great practical exercises which really encourage you to think about who you are, what you want, where you're heading and why? This book will really help you on your way.

Gerry McNulty, Writer/Performer

The Strengths Way is a great book that mixes the theoretical with the practical in a way that makes the subject accessible to anyone. The book contains many case studies of people that have decided to 'live the dream' and follow their passions, often taking great risks, with inspiring results. The strengths approach described in the book also works superbly inside established companies that seek to harness the abilities of their people. I have seen it at first hand – and it works!

Vice President, Human Resources Europe , Sony Europe

For a complete list of Management Books 2000 titles
visit our web-site on http://www.mb2000.com

The
Strengths
Way

The art of
building on strengths

Mike Pegg

2000

First published in 2006 by Management Books 2000 Ltd
Forge House, Limes Road
Kemble, Cirencester
Gloucestershire, GL7 6AD, UK
Tel: 0044 (0) 1285 771441
Fax: 0044 (0) 1285 771055
Email: info@mb2000.com
Web: www.mb2000.com

Printed and bound in Great Britain by 4edge Ltd of Hockley, Essex – www.4edge.co.uk

British Library Cataloguing in Publication Data is available

ISBN 9781852525422

Contents

Introduction

The Strengths Way is a positive way of working with people. It helps people to build on their strengths, set specific goals and achieve success. People can follow their vocation, find the right vehicle and do valuable work. They can flow, focus, finish and, as a by-product, find fulfilment. They may need to be both 'soul-wise' and 'street wise', because making things happen sometimes calls for being quite 'savvy'. People can follow their passion, translate it into a clear purpose and achieve peak performance. They can pass on their knowledge and sometimes experience a sense of peace.

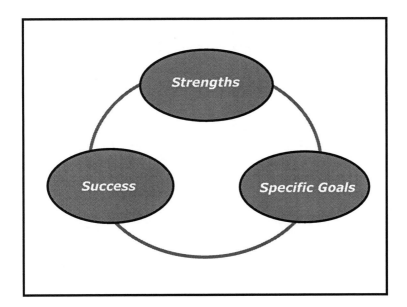

The Strengths Way is about encouragement. It is about how we can use our strengths to help others to succeed. One of the reasons we are here is to encourage present and future generations. Forty years ago I was fortunate enough to given the opportunity to work with people. At the time I was very idealistic – and today I have an even greater belief in people. They have taught me three things.

First: *People can choose their spirit – their attitude to life.*

They can choose to be positive or negative, creators or complainers. People can focus on what they can control, rather than complain about what they can't control. Writing in *Man's Search For Meaning,* Viktor Frankl described his nightmare journey through the Nazi concentration camps. He found that many survivors had something to live for beyond the immediate terror. They had a book to write, a relationship to rebuild or a dream to pursue. Viktor wrote: "Man is not free from his conditions, but he is free to take a stand towards his conditions." Everybody makes choices – and each choice has consequences.

Second: *People can build on their strengths, set specific goals and work hard to achieve their picture of success.*

Everybody is an artist, everybody is creative. Everybody has something special to give to the world. Everybody can find activities in which they deliver A's, rather than B's or C's. During the past 40 years I have worked with people from many walks of life – troubled teenagers, educators, business leaders, knowledge workers, artists, sports people and many super teams. Everybody I have met has had natural gifts. People can be offered tools they can use to make full use of their talents.

Third: *People can use their strengths to serve others and help them to achieve success.*

"You are most yourself when you forget yourself," we are told. Life is about finding yourself, accepting yourself and forgetting yourself. Alec Dickson, one of my mentors, believed in the importance of service – and felt the giver got as much as the receiver. He founded

Voluntary Service Overseas and Community Service Volunteers. CSV gave me the opportunity to become a housefather for mentally handicapped children. Since that day I have always had the opportunity to do fulfilling work. People go through the stages of gathering experience, making sense of experience and passing-on experience. Everybody can use their talents to help others and build a more positive planet. Let's explore how a person can use their gifts.

Step 1: Strengths

Everybody can find activities in which they quickly reach 7/10. The challenge is to find a niche in which they consistently achieve at least a 9/10. So how can you, for example, identify your 'A' talent? One approach is to focus on three themes: a) Your strengths – which is what you do best; b) Your successful style – which is how you work best; c) Your special contribution – which is combining your strengths and successful style to clarify your best contribution. You can find your talents by using questions such as:

"What are the activities in which you deliver A's, rather than B's or C's? When do you feel in your element – at ease and yet able to excel? When do you quickly see the destination – the picture of perfection? When do you go 'A, B...then jump to....Z'? Where do you quickly see patterns? What is your successful style of working? Looking back on your life, what for you have been satisfying 'projects'? What did you do right then? How can you follow these principles more in the future? How can you combine your strengths and successful style to clarify your special contribution?"

Step 2: Specific Goals

Everybody can set specific goals. So how can you, for example, clarify your picture of perfection? If you wish, you can focus on three themes: a) You can set specific goals; b) You can, if appropriate, find potential sponsors (a sponsor is somebody who may hire you for doing what you do best); c) You can clarify your strategy for achieving your specific goals. One approach is to use questions such as:

"What is your picture of success? Imagine you are looking back at your life when you are 80. What will be the 3 things you will have done that for you will mean your life has been successful? What do you want to pass on to other people? If you want to get paid for doing what you love, how can you find potential sponsors? What are the key challenges they face? How can you help them to succeed? Once you have found sponsors, how can you make clear working contracts? Let's return to your life-time goals and legacy. What are the 3 key strategies you can pursue to give yourself the greatest chance of success?"

Step 3: Success

Everybody can work hard to achieve their picture of perfection. Peak performers develop good habits, for example, and do the right things in the right way every day. Overcoming setbacks, they work hard until they reach their goals. Sometimes they then also add that 'touch of class'. Here are four steps you may wish to consider on your journey: a) You can do superb work; b) You can find solutions to challenges; c) You can help other people to succeed; d) You can achieve your picture of success. How to chart your route toward reaching your goals? One approach is to use questions such as:

"How can you do superb work? How can you follow the daily disciplines? How can you satisfy your sponsors? How can you encourage yourself along the journey? How can you anticipate and manage any setbacks? How can you find creative solutions to challenges? How can you stay proactive and keep tackling issues that are in the green, amber and red zones? How can you use your strengths to help others to succeed? How can you be a good finisher? How can you do everything possible to achieve the picture of perfection? How can you keep improving? How can you help to build a more positive planet?"

Encouragement, Enterprise & Excellence

How can we help people to build on their strengths? One approach is to learn from great educators. They focus on encouragement, enterprise and excellence. After providing an encouraging environment, they look for when the person shows enterprise and work with them to achieve excellence. Great educators also focus on inspiration, implementation and integration. After creating an inspiring environment, they provide implementation tools that work. They then enable people to integrate the learning in their own way. Great educators help people to expand their repertoire of choices. People then have more models, knowledge and tools they can use to achieve success.

"Sounds okay in theory, but how does it work in practice?" somebody may say. "Will it work with all people in all situations?" So far we have looked at the 'soft' side of encouraging people – let's move onto the 'hard' side. People can reach their goals provided they are prepared to focus on:

a) Clarity

People need to clarify the 'What' before moving onto the 'How'. They need to focus on the real results they want to achieve and clarify their picture of perfection.

b) Contracting

People need to make clear contracts that they are prepared to work hard to reach the goals. They must make these contracts first with themselves and second, where appropriate, with other people. When asked: "On scale 0 – 10, how serious are you about reaching your goals?" the answer needs to be at least 9/10. People buy benefits. They will only set-out on a journey if they believe they will get more pluses than minuses by achieving the goal.

c) *Concrete Results*

People must get quick successes. They will then gain the self-confidence required to pursue their chosen strategies, overcome setbacks and keep working hard to achieve the picture of perfection.

The Strengths Way is a positive way. People want more than theory, however, they want practical tools that work. So the book includes many stories from individuals who have translated the principles into practice. Take the ideas you like and use them in your own way. Good luck in continuing to build on your own and other people's strengths.

STEP 1:

STRENGTHS

"Everybody is an artist; everybody is creative." That was my mantra when I began working with people. During the early years I worked in therapeutic communities for people who had been given 'labels' – such as delinquent, neurotic, schizophrenic and 'maladjusted'. In 1976 I began teaching five day courses in 'Strengths Building' – which led to working with knowledge workers, business leaders, football managers and super teams. Whatever the person's 'label', the key was to build on their strengths.

"But what about a person's personality – doesn't that play a part?" somebody may ask. Absolutely. People who shape their future have a certain kind of 'spirit'. Choosing to be positive rather than negative, they recognise that: 'Attitude plus ability equals achievement.' People do not choose their talents but, providing they are given the basic materials for life, they do choose how to use their talents.

Sue Carter is such a person. In 1970 she came to the therapeutic community I was running for young people. Abandoned by her mother at the age of 2, she had grown up suffering abuse in institutions. The community gave young people the chance to shape their futures. Sue recognised she was at a crossroads and began pursuing her chosen route. Putting her troubles behind her, she aimed to do one thing in life – to be a good parent. In 2005, quite out of the blue, she emailed me to describe her journey over the past three decades. Sue was always feisty, which shines through her story *My Aim To Be A Good Parent*. Visited later in life by the Essex police who were investigating events at the children's homes, the police asked if she was a victim of abuse. Sue declared: "No, I am a survivor of abuse."

My Aim To Be A Good Parent

Sue Carter

My mother abandoned me and my two sisters in the park when I was two. During the next 14 years I moved from one children's home to another. Sometimes I was abused but I did not know anything else, so I thought it was normal. One housefather kept hitting me with his belt, so I yelled: "Why are you hitting me?" He said it was because I needed to show him respect. I yelled back: "I'm not going to respect you if you keep hitting me." So he hit me harder.

One day I found myself in an institution that was famous for holding a girl who had killed a child. Looking back, I now realize that the only way I had kept my sanity was by rebelling, but it had got me into trouble. Things looked bad, but then I got the chance to go to a community where young people like me had the opportunity to change their lives. Over 30 years later I now have three sons and a wonderful granddaughter, who is the apple of my eye. The 30 years in-between have sometimes been difficult, but never dull. After leaving the community I met a man and travelled around the world. Returning home, I began working in a children's home. Growing-up in institutions myself, I knew what the children needed and tried to help them to feel safe and loved. Even if I say it myself, I found that I was good with children.

During my twenties I had several long relationships and eventually got married. Unfortunately my husband tried to control me. Even if I was going to Sainsbury's, he wanted to know what I was doing. I was never one to let anyone control me, so end of marriage. Eventually I realised that I didn't have good relationships with men because I tested them to the limit. So I wasn't shocked when they didn't reach my expectations. And, of course, I also made some bad choices.

My greatest fear as a parent was that my kids could end up in care. So I then decided to be the best single parent I could be. This meant relationships with men were out. I stayed on my own with the boys for the next 18 years. Then I met a good man with whom I had a child.

Even though the man and I have now parted, we are still good friends and he is a good father.

Looking back at my time in the community, I am so happy that I was given the opportunity to meet people who taught me it was okay to talk about things. So much pain was bottled up inside me from the years spent in care and the abuse that I and my sisters suffered. I was one of the lucky ones. I found a way to confront my demons, talk about them and they stopped hurting. About 10 years ago my sisters and I were contacted by the police about the abuse we experienced in children's homes. The police came to my house and met with me and my sisters and asked if we were victims of abuse. I stood up, faced the policeman and said "NO, I AM A SURVIVOR OF ABUSE."

Then I realised I had got rid of my demons. Some people never get the chance to rid themselves of past problems. Looking back, the community showed there were people who could look after kids, value their opinions and not resort to abuse. The community made us feel safe and we never betrayed that trust. Some newcomers tried to bring drugs into the house, but we said: 'Don't bring that stuff here. If you want to take drugs, leave the community.'

Sometimes we had fantastic talks. There would be 8 of us sitting in a bedroom till midnight, just sharing thoughts we had never discussed with anybody before. Every young person in the community had suffered problems. We encouraged each other to talk about the past, but didn't allow each other to use it as an excuse for behaving badly. If I said, 'My mother left me in the park when I was two,' somebody else said: 'I can top that. How can you use that bad experience to help others in the future?'

Suddenly I realised that I didn't have to go on the path I was hurtling along, which would probably have led to drugs or prison. The people in the community believed in us and my feelings mattered. Someone listened when I was screaming. What could be more wonderful than that? Nowadays I try to help other people by volunteering to work at the local hospice. But the thing I am most proud of is being a good parent to my children.

The Strengths Way contains stories from people who, like Sue, have chosen to retake control of their lives. So how can you express your talents – especially in the world of work? There are no jobs any more – there are only projects. So it is important to think like a freelancer – even if you work in an organisation. One approach is to focus on: a) Your strengths – which is what you do best; b) Your successful style – which is how you work best; c) Your special contribution – which is combining your strengths and successful style to clarify your best contribution to an employer. Let's explore these steps.

a) *You can clarify your strengths*

How to discover what you do best? You may want to read the piece called *Fifty Ways To Find Your Strengths.* This provides many ideas for exploring your talents. But how do these work in practice? Let's look at some people who have brought these themes to life.

Steve Morris follows his passion – which is writing – and translates this into peak performance. He is the co-founder of Burton Morris – a specialist language company that helps major brands to find their true voice. Steve has worked with companies such as M&S, Boots, Lloyds TSB, British Airways and Norwich Union. So how did he become a full-time writer? Steve's story can be found in the piece called *My Passion: Doing work I love.* The kick-start came from being made redundant by his employers. He writes:

"This was my chance to put my passion for words to use. I got a computer, set it up in the spare room and haven't had an enforced day without writing for 13 years…The first customer came through a recommendation. Then another recommendation…"

Fifty Ways To Find Your Strengths

Here are some clues to finding your strengths. Some are simply starting points for exploration and there are many overlaps between the themes. You may want to combine some themes to clarify your top talents.

You can focus on the specific activities in which:

1. *You consistently deliver A's, rather than B's or C's. You build on you A's and manage the consequences of your B's and C's.*

2. *You do something you feel passionately about. You follow your passion, translate it into a clear purpose and deliver peak performance. Sometimes you find a sense of peace.*

3. *You do what you enjoy. You feel fully alive and alert. You are living the vital life, rather than the vanilla life.*

4. *You feel in your element – you are at ease and yet also excel. You have a natural 'feel' for this activity and find that 'things come easily'. You feel 'at home' in the situation.*

5. *You get positive energy, rather than negative energy. You feel excited just thinking about the activity. You feel positively engaged, rather than partly engaged or pretend engaged.*

6. *You get 'creative highs'. Your whole body changes, you become captivated and get a creative kick from doing the work.*

7. *You are extremely calm in situations that others may find difficult. You are calm, clear and deliver concrete results. You deliver peak performance without feeling pressure.*

8. *You eagerly anticipate the 'big occasions'. You say: "I can't wait for it to happen." You are confident you will do your best. You are able to flow, rather than fear.*

9. *You quickly get to 7/10. You are then able to make the exponential climb from 7/10 to 10/10.*

10. *You see the destination quickly and clarify the potential picture of perfection. You go 'A, B...then leap to...Z'.*

11. *You see patterns quickly. You extrapolate the patterns to predict what will happen. You build on the successful patterns, minimise the self-defeating patterns and work hard to achieve success.*

12. *You have 'personal radar' – a term coined by Al Siebert, author of The Survivor personality – and you 'know what will happen before it happens'.*

13. *You employ your radar and have the repertoire required to deliver the right results.*

14. *You make complicated things simple. You get to the heart of the matter. You demonstrate the 'second simplicity' – which is a profound simplicity.*

15. *You are simultaneously both 'helicoptering' and 'hands-on'. You hover above the situation and see the key patterns. At the same time you are 'hands-on' and feel able to directly shape what is happening in front of you.*

16. *You experience a sense of 'flow' – a term used by Mihaly Csikszentmihaly, the author of Flow. You flow, focus, finish and, as a by-product, find fulfilment.*

17. *You go into your equivalent of the 'zone'. You find that things go 'slowly but speedily'.*

18. *You balance seeming paradoxes. You simultaneously see the big picture and have attention to detail. You move easily between the concept and the concrete, the philosophical and the practical.*

19. *You score highly on drive, detail and delivery. You have a strong drive, great attention to detail and you deliver. You score at least 8/10 in each category.*

20. *You have the equivalent of a photographic memory in this activity. If you are an athlete or dancer, for example, your*

equivalent will be 'muscle memory'. You have almost total recall of specific situations.

21. You continually practice mental rehearsal. You relax, rehearse and deliver the right results.

22. You are fascinated by the subject and daydream about the activity. You continually explore potential future scenarios. You have a 'memory of the future' – a term coined by Arie de Guis, author of The Living Company.

23. You love making decisions in this activity and you make good quality decisions. You clarify the challenges, choices, consequences, creative solutions and conclusions – then make good decisions.

24. You have the 'will' as well as the skill required to reach the goal. You score highly on each stage of 'the achievement model': attitude, ability, application, adventure and achievement.

25. You are naturally self-disciplined. You keep doing the right things in the right way to get the right results. You get the right balance between consistency and creativity.

26. You enjoy doing the grunt work as well as the great work. You enjoy the sweat on the road to success.

27. You are resilient and quickly overcome setbacks. You learn from difficulties and emerge stronger. Sometimes the setbacks provide the springboard for making new breakthroughs.

28. You adopt the positive approach, rather than the percentage or paralysis approach. You focus on the 'top, rather than the drop'.

29. You really care about what you are doing. You score at least 9/10 on the caring dimension. You put a lot of love into the work.

30. You have a sense of service – as if you are serving something greater than yourself. Sometimes you feel as if you are 'channelling' the energy towards achieving a specific goal.

31. *You put yourself in the background and have no ego. You commit yourself fully to helping other people or the 'project' to succeed – which releases your creativity. You recognise that 'you are most yourself when you forget yourself'.*

32. *You enjoy the journey as much as reaching the goal. You enjoy the process as much as achieving the prize.*

33. *You experience a sense of play – but you know there is nothing as serious as play. You feel free to adventure and explore. You are able to try things without the fear of making mistakes – which means that you often make new discoveries.*

34. *You are a good finisher. You have a track record of finishing things in this activity. So you feel confident you will be able to do whatever is necessary to finish.*

35. *You get the right balance between design, development and delivery. You design things that are simple, beautiful and effective.*

36. *You feel that you are using the 'best' part of yourself. You feel generous and want to pass on your knowledge. You want to help other people to succeed.*

37. *You follow your successful style. Everybody has a positive history – a way they work best – and you are following your preferred way. You are pursuing 'What' you do best and 'How' you work best.*

38. *You are working on the right 'project' with the right people in the right place. It scores high on the stimulation factor. You are doing a stimulating project, with stimulating people in a stimulating place.*

39. *You get the right balance between innovation, implementation and impact. You can be innovative, implement ideas and make a positive impact.*

40. *You follow your values, translate these into a clear vision and deliver visible results.*

41. *You are doing your soul work, rather than salary work. You do work that involves your heart, hands and head.*

42. *You feel you are following your 'tradition'. People have trodden this path in the past and others will pursue in the future. You feel part of that tradition.*

43. *You are a 'warrior-wizard'. Warriors work hard and always deliver 8/10. Warrior-wizards also work hard, but add that touch of magic to produce the 10/10.*

44. *You are a pacesetter and make the 'new rules for the game'. You are a 'deviant who delivers'. You do things your own way yet deliver great work.*

45. *You are positive, professional and a peak performer. You are doing what you do best and doing it brilliantly. You do work that is of 'high value and hard to replace'.*

46. *You give superb customer service. You work with your 'perfect customer', understand their agenda and help them to achieve success.*

47. *You 'surf the sigmoid curve'. You continually keep developing – moving from one level to the next level.*

48. *You constantly want to learn and develop. You are committed to constant improvement.*

49. *You can become a class act in this activity. You do superb work to reach the goal – then add that touch of class.*

50. *You feel you are following your vocation. You feel: 'This is what I was meant to do.' You follow your vocation, find the right 'vehicle' and do valuable work.*

My Passion: Doing work I love
Steve Morris

I always wanted to be a writer. Well from at least the age of about 7. My mother read to me and I was always making up stories. I was bookish. And to me earning a living from writing seemed a noble thing to do. I kept thinking it would be wonderful not to have a proper job. Especially as my father was a carpet fitter, and that kind of thing looked really difficult.

I think I realised very early on that writing was my 'A' strength. Partly it was because I really enjoyed doing it. But also I seemed to learn quite quickly. Even by about the age of 12, I was pretty sure that writing was what I was good at. It helped that I was so rubbish at just about everything else. I've never been able to do as much as put a plug on. I am completely impractical, other than when writing about practical things.

So I was clear early on, that for the sake of everyone else's safety I should stick with the words.

This gave me a game plan. Develop my writing skills and don't stop until I'm earning a living from it.

After the English degree and post grad study I worked as an editor, which was fine. I learned a huge amount from my boss Liz Dunbar (we still work together). That red pen inflicted pain, but boy did I learn how things should be done. Second job was as managing editor. Different place, different learning. Here it was about managing writers and taking responsibility. And then something happened. The money ran out for the organisation and we were all made redundant.

This was my chance to put my passion for words to use. I got a computer, set it up in the spare room and haven't had an enforced day without writing for 13 years.

But it was in working for myself that a greater sense of purpose came. I had always believed in the power of words. Lazy writing,

23

jargon, clichés annoyed me. I realised that I wasn't selling writing. I was actually selling the dream that words can add craft and fun and that organisations that sound dead are dead.

The first customer came through a recommendation. Then another recommendation. People move on and when they do they ask you to come and work some magic in their new place of work.

I began to realise that I could make connections. That I could see the big picture and that I could explain just why a certain phrase was right and another would be wrong. I began working with major brands helping them to find their voice. It was pioneering work and without being immodest my peers in the industry have often said that my work has taken our understanding of language and brands to a new level.

To genuinely develop the 'A' strength you need to see just how widely you can learn about it. I realised that I had to get better at developing ideas. I know now that I just need to let ideas come to me. That I should not force them. That if I give myself space I can see the big picture. So I don't think about problem-solving, I just keep going back to first principles and the answers are there:

- *Think of the reader*
- *Enjoy words*
- *Choose the right medium*
- *Read it back to yourself*
- *Hear the conversation and then write it down.*

Simple stuff really.

The thing is that writing still gives me a great sense of fulfilment. I like feeling free on the page. I like taking nothing and adding words so that you have something. I love it when we take a brand that writes in a bureaucratic and inconsistent way and really help that brand to write in a more contemporary and relevant way. I like it when you go into a company and a short time later people are talking about language, enjoying words and improving their own writing skills. For me, good writing is a joy and being able to write well is one of the top life skills.

I work with companies that I like to shop with and so I get a sense of fulfilment when those companies write to me in a human, engaging way. It is bringing about change that I like as much as words.

I have really mined my one great talent. I was lucky because I realised it was what I was good at. And I was good at it because I enjoyed it and my brain worked in the right way. Whenever I've tried to use the 'B', 'C' and 'D' skills I have failed and been unhappy into to bargain. These days I only use my 'A' game. That's it.

Charlie Duggan also does work he loves, but also in a place he loves. His vocation is helping other people to succeed and the vehicle he uses is his own recruitment agency. Charlie helps people to find jobs that create a 'win-win' for both themselves and their employer. Several years ago he faced a challenge: "I am doing it for other people – so perhaps I ought to also do it for myself." Charlie lived in Bristol and worked for a good employer – but most of his days were spent near London. The daily commute ate into his energy until one day he decided to set-up his own firm in Bristol. What provided the trigger? You can find the answer in his piece called *Santa's Little Helper.*

I am fortunate to have one of the best jobs in the world – helping people build on their strengths. During the late 60s and early 70s I spent hours in the London bookshops, scouring the shelves for books about people's talents. Eventually I found writers like Abraham Maslow, Carl Rogers, Viktor Frankl, Virginia Satir, John Dewey, Sylvia Ashton-Warner and Virginia Axline – then people such as Richard Bolles, George Dennison, David Wills, Henry Pluckrose, Barrie Hopson and Mike Scally. Tony Manocchio, an outstanding therapist, provided ongoing encouragement and got me the job running the therapeutic community for young people. During this period I also met George Lyward, a pioneer in child care.

George achieved outstanding results at Finchden Manor – a community for disturbed boys. Bus loads of social workers travelled into the Kent countryside to visit Finchden to seek the secret of his success. Walking around the community, they saw boys playing guitars, kicking footballs, building sheds, planting flowers and reading. Finally the visitors crammed into the hall and bombarded George with questions. They asked: "What therapy do you believe in? What is the staff's role? They seem to do little except watch the boys."

Santa's Helper

Charlie Duggan

What does it take to set you on your journey? It took a trip to a primary school Christmas fair to set me on mine. The moment my wife, Vick, appeared from behind the tinsel curtain of Santa's grotto dressed as an elf, I was well and truly on my way. The excited chirrups and bustle around me melted away. A moment of piercing sky blue clarity overcame me. Enough was enough. It was time to resign.

18 months earlier Vick had made the life-changing decision to retrain and qualify as a teacher – no mean feat when you consider that our girls were then aged 2 and 4 and I was spending increasing time working away from home. Juggling full-time university and childcare was going to require careful planning and budgeting. But it was what she passionately wanted to do and I was going to support her in every way I could.

Fast forward to the Christmas fair and there she was firmly yet gently working and bantering on a first name basis with the grotto queue. I felt immensely proud of her. Here was first hand evidence that she had realised her dream, worked to her strengths and managed to plan her family life around her. She looked genuinely fulfilled. Now it was my turn.

I spent that weekend churning ideas over in my mind, trying to work out what was important to me as a father, a husband and an employee and what gave me the zip to jump out of bed in the morning. Vick had given me the emotional push to make a big leap. I owed it to both her and myself to make it a bold step.

I spent my three months' 'gardening leave' recharging my batteries. No point rushing things – I had to make sure my 'bold step' was a step in the right direction, one that would give me and my family more time together. For the first time in 4 years I got as excited as the girls during the run up to Christmas. Their enthusiasm was infectious. They had always served as instant 'stress-busters' after a long working week, but now they had earned themselves a new title – energy-givers.

Who better to go to in a time of need than my best man, Tim? Together we came up with mad-cap schemes and more sensible business ideas. I also sought wisdom in the entrepreneurial section of my local bookshop, racing through 'Beer mat Entrepreneur', 'Anyone Can Do It' and 'Who Says Elephants Can't dance?' I really was beginning to enjoy myself.

By the New Year, I had pretty much decided that I wanted to create something myself, free of corporate baggage. Some sort of niche start up allowing me to exploit a gap in the market and put my years of experience in the recruitment industry to good use. On the last day of my gardening leave, it was with a sense of occasion and a little trepidation that I dropped my laptop back to the Bristol office. I was going it alone. Three days later, whilst making my first business development calls, my ex-CEO rang with news of their latest client win. Would I be interested in helping them get the contract operational? Bingo! My first sale! A week later, arriving back in the office as Managing Consultant of my own, spanking new business. I could not help but smile as they handed me back my old laptop. Charlie Duggan Associates was up and running.

"The staff members are talent spotters," said George. "They look for when the boy 'comes alive'. The boy may be painting, playing football or whatever. The staff members then help the boy to create more of those golden moments in their lives. Watching people is one of the hardest jobs in world. Our task is to help each boy to find his true work in life."

Reflecting back on my own life, I have been fortunate to have had many Encouragers. My parents adopted me when I was a few weeks old. They provided constant encouragement, even though I was no good at school. Reflecting on the 6 years I spent working in a factory, I was fortunate to eventually meet a teacher who opened the doors to a new world. Along with my fellow apprentices, I spent 2 days a month at the local Technical College. One afternoon Mr Smitman, the Social Studies teacher, asked us to write an essay about George Orwell's *1984*. Returning the essays one month later, he had written on my paper: "See me after class." Mr Smitman explained that he taught GCE English at night school. "You can come along to the class and, if you want, study for the examination next year," he said. "Whatever you do in the future, I am sure you won't be in a factory for the rest of your life."

Community Services Volunteers eventually gave me the chance to do work I loved. So I am biased. I believe everybody is an artist, everybody is creative. The great teachers I met showed it was possible for people to use their talents. Encouragement is the foundation for enabling people to show enterprise and work towards achieving excellence.

Let's imagine you have found your talents (There are many exercises on this theme at the end of this chapter.) The next step is to clarify the best way to translate these into action.

b) *You can clarify your successful style*

Your strengths are 'What' you do best. Your style is 'How' you work best. Putting the two together provides a powerful combination. How to discover the key? During the 70s and 80s I learned a lot from sports psychology. Based in Scandinavia at the time, I was running 5 day Strength Building courses for people from all walks of life, whilst also giving guest lectures at the national sports universities. Great sports psychologists invite athletes to revisit their best performances. The athlete clarifies what they did right and how they can follow these principles in the future. You can adopt a similar approach by studying your own positive history. If you wish, you can tackle the exercise on this theme called *My Successful Style.*

Start by looking back on your life. What for you have been the most satisfying 'projects'? Use the word 'project' in its widest sense. You may have passed an exam, travelled around Europe, designed a web site, run a marathon, shipped a product, written an article, led a team or whatever. Looking at each project in turn, what made each one satisfying? Can you see any recurring patterns? Bearing these in mind, try to describe your successful style. You may have two preferred ways of working. One when you are working by yourself, one when working with other people.

Alison Fulford knows the way she works best. She has a great track record of leading high impact projects for businesses – especially those that provide superb customer service. She prefers a two year 'project' – but within that time frame also builds a self-managing team that sustains the good work. Alison spent her early working years at Microsoft, then moved onto consultancy but found it frustrating. Why?

"My kicks come from getting my hands dirty, working hard and seeing tangible results, especially in improving customer satisfaction," says Alison. "Impact is important. I want to build something that works for both the company and the customer. Finally, it is crucial to recruit my successor and ensure the improvements are sustainable. Only then will I move on to the next project."

Alison is brilliant at customer service. She has the ability to design systems that please the customer yet also make money for the company. A leading UK retailer spotted this talent and invited her to set up a new Service Centre – one that actually provided great customer service. She describes what happened in her piece called

Making It Special For Customers. Mission accomplished, Alison moved-on after two years to leading another high impact project.

Different people prefer to work in different ways. One medical researcher said: "I work best as a sole contributor in situations where: a) I really believe in the project; b) I feel it can improve the quality of people's lives; c) I can have some input into the 'What' – the results to achieve; d) I work for a manager with whom I can have a dialogue; e) I have reasonable freedom on how to conduct the research; f) I must produce a visible product – such as a paper for a journal. Medical research is a competitive field. So it's vital for me to publish to increase the possibility of finding future exciting assignments."

Making it Special for Customers

Alison Fulford

I love shopping. More specifically, I love buying. But what makes me buy? It is when the whole experience feels great. So wonderful that I want to go back time after time after time. (Is this an addiction, I ask? Oh well, it is extremely enjoyable.) Over the years I have become fascinated by how to provide great experiences for customers.

Two years ago I was asked to put this principle into practice. One of the country's leading retailers asked me to design their new service centre. What an opportunity! Within 18 months we were getting superb feedback inside and outside the company. So what happened? Looking back, the key principles we followed were:

1)   Find out what matters to your customers.
2)   Craft your picture of perfection which describes your vision.
3)   Recruit people who can fulfil the vision.
...then make it happen!

Sounds common-sense and every self-respecting company will sign-up to these sentiments – but how to put them into practice? I started by finding out about our customers. First, who were they? The obvious people were those who visited our shops. But there were many others. For example, the business leaders, the people who work in the stores and so on.

So I set-off to talk to people in the stores. They wanted help to serve their customers better. Sometimes it was practical help – such as getting the resources required to give great customer service. Sometimes it was just someone to call who could help them to solve a customer problem. Then I talked with the business leaders. They wanted to improve the sales, reduce costs and enhance the company's reputation. The shoppers stated their wishes clearly.

a)   They wanted to find the products they wanted easily and, of course, buy them when they wanted.

b)   They wanted the 'personal touch'. For example, if they had a problem, they wanted help to be available. If they had a query, they wanted to feel listened to and important. Most of all, they wanted someone to take them seriously and take ownership for solving the problem.

Something was still missing. So far we were simply tackling the basics. Our aim must be to make shopping memorable – in a positive way! If people felt special, they'd want to buy from us more. And they might also tell their friends about the great experiences in our stores. Imagine what it would be like if every customer was able to speak to a real person - someone who listened carefully and actually held a conversation with them. Supposing we worked with our customers to agree a way forward that satisfied the customer and served the business. Supposing we talked in plain English and tried not to use our own jargon.

Returning to the service centre, I began talking in these terms. Everybody must understand we were creating a service centre – not a call centre. It was about helping people, not about transacting 'incidents'. Our people must be approachable, human, honest, genuine and interested – plus being problem solvers. On occasions, we might need to say "No," but communicate the 'bad news' in a respectful way that left customers feeling good about that decision. Sounds impossible? Perhaps, but we aimed to be superb, especially during the difficult moments.

The early days were frustrating. 'Old school' advocates explained how things had always been done, rather than explore the new possibilities in the new world. Some felt more comfortable with hard measures, such as how many telephone calls were answered each hour, rather than the percentage of customers who were actually satisfied. As the leader, mine was the final call. So I simply asked people to try a new way of thinking and a new way of serving customers. Within weeks, no one wanted to go back to the old way.

People probably thought I was mad at first. But, like a broken record, I kept talking about serving customers, not transacting phone calls. Every project has a pivotal moment – when things come together or fall apart. Our turning point came when I created – then communicated – the picture of perfection. Looking into the future, I described what the service centre would look like when it was working beautifully. Drawing a picture of this world, I even called it Planet Perfection. Involving key people, we listed what our customers would see, do and hear. Then we described our future experience of working in the service centre.

On Planet Perfection, we would receive more than 'Thank you,' letters. Customers would write specific positive words about how they felt after experiencing our service. Our teams would buzz from solving problems – sharing information and knowledge to help each other succeed. We would never walk past a quality issue. Our business leaders would feel proud of us and see tangible results. People would aspire to work in the service centre – there would be a queue into the car park. We would only measure things that helped us improve and, of course, celebrate success.

After describing Planet Perfection, everything became much easier. Breaking all my rules, because I believe in living the values, rather than simply laminating the values, I even carried around a copy of the picture. Meeting people, I walked them through the vision, so they clearly understood our goals. Interviewing the core team became exciting. Starting with the picture of perfection, I asked what they could do to help make it happen. The response was amazing. People offered all kinds of experience and skills. Relishing creating something different, everyone was a volunteer. After hiring the core team – and getting the systems in place – we were ready for lift-off. We must recruit the right people – around 100 of them – to make the new service centre fly.

"Recruiting will be a challenge," we were told, "because this is an area with less than 2% unemployment." After talking with many agencies, we selected two. They were positive, action oriented and very customer focused. At the agency briefing, I started with the picture of perfection, not even mentioning job profiles and pay. Within minutes, the successful agencies were describing the kind of people we'd need to make the picture of perfection happen. They understood completely what we needed and set off to find the right people.

Meeting the candidates, we shared the vision – then asked how they might be able to contribute. Listening as they talked, we looked for three signs. First, they needed to be excited about the vision. Second, they needed to demonstrate how they would help us to *achieve the picture. Third, beneath it all, they must have the desire to make the experience special for our customers. The process was enlightening. Fortunately, we found many people with varied strengths who could deliver different elements of the vision.*

The team was recruited; the energy levels were sky high – and the results were stunning. Soon our picture became a reality. Previously, for example, complaining customers had been sent an acknowledgement, coupled with a gift voucher. We found that a sincere apology for a mistake went a long way to solving the problem. Our costs started to drop significantly and, within 6 months, more than 50% of the 'thank you,' letters received referred to how we had dealt with customers' issues. Leaders from the business asked to visit our service centre – as did customer service directors from other companies. Grabbing the opportunity, we also took their good ideas and integrated these into our business.

Great work begins by getting the basics right. Such an approach may not appeal to some companies that are looking for a 'magic bullet', but this is what we aimed to do. On top of this, we could then add something special. Looking back, then, we took three steps.

1) *We found out what was needed by simply talking with internal and external customers. People who dealt with customers every day described their common problems and the desired solutions. They became the real architects of the work.*

2) *We created a vivid picture of the service centre and recruited the right people. They found it helpful to have this vision and 'volunteered-in' to make it happen.*

3) *We found that continually revisiting the picture of perfection enabled people to stay on track. Returning to the picture – yet also seeing it evolve – helped everybody to agree on the roles and rules for working together and getting the right results. Then we made it happen.*

Creating the service centre was deeply satisfying. People who chose to be part of it said they felt valued – which is a feeling they transmitted to their customers. And does it beat shopping? I will pass on that one, but it is very fulfilling to help other people feel special.

Simon Walker knows his successful style. He loves to lead motivated people towards tackling an inspiring challenge that also helps them to develop as individuals. He took this step when skippering 'Toshiba' in the BT Global Challenge round-the-world race in 1996. You can read his story in the piece called *Racing Around The World*. At 28 years old, he was the youngest ever skipper, with some crew members being twice his age. Certainly he had the 'technical' experience. Simon had sailed the Atlantic Ocean 7 times, led two expeditions to the Arctic Ocean, won the first Teacher's Whiskey Round Britain Challenge race and been first mate on an earlier BT Global Challenge. But did he have the people skills?

Simon is passionate about building great teams. He has a very 'humanistic' leadership style which combines top-notch professionalism with the ability to give clear messages. His greatest gift is educating people to become self-managing. After completing the 1996/97 race, he became Managing Director of the Challenge Business. Seven years later he moved on to running his own business. Simon's piece gives an insight into how the crew developed before and during the race. No, they didn't win, they came second – but they achieved something equally lasting that was included in their picture of perfection. Simon writes:

"At the end of the race we had all 'grown'. There are many stories – people have gone to greater things in sailing, but mostly people have used it as a springboard in 'life', using the self knowledge to give them a confidence and perspective which is hard to match. And looking back, what were the 'take away' lessons? One above all: Enjoy it. Otherwise you have missed the point, which is probably the same rule in life."

Let's imagine you know 'What' you do best and 'How' you work best. It's time to move onto the next step. Anybody can do work they love, the art is getting somebody to pay you for doing it. Let's explore how to make this happen.

Racing Around the World
Simon Walker

I have always loved building teams. Many of these have been when sailing – others have been onshore in business. The following pages describe building a team that raced around the world – and the key part was making sure that everybody agreed on the specific goals.

Racing yachts across the oceans has occupied much of my life. Every detail and challenge has excited me. So when I was appointed skipper of "Toshiba" in the 1996/97 BT Global Challenge, I entered a project for which I felt a deep passion. Four years earlier I had been lucky enough to race around the world. Since that time I had visualised every inch of the course. For example, I pictured reaching Rio in every conceivable circumstance – in the day, night, rough and calm weather. When we finally sailed into Rio in a very close 2nd place, it felt 'normal', as if we had done it a thousand times. But let's go back to the beginning.

The BT Global Challenge is different from other races. People with mixed levels of sailing experience apply for the 10 month race around the world. Some stay for the full journey; others take part in one of the legs and are called 'Leggers'. The skippers are chosen ahead of time, but the crews are selected into 'balanced' teams by the race organisers. This 'balance' is based on skills, age, gender, mix and personality type. So what makes the difference? During the previous Global Challenge, we discovered that each boat's performance had to do with the skippers' ability to develop the full potential of their teams. Ultimately, the race was all about managing people. So, after being allocated your crew, how do you build them into a great team?

Different skippers have different approaches. Some immediately go out onto the water; others spend time charting the course ahead. Immediately after my crew was selected, I arranged for us to get together in a large unheated house in rural Wales. This was 8 months before the starting gun fired and long before we ever got to sail the yacht. where they spent two days talking about the race. You can't build a team before you've agreed on the goal. As the leader, I explained my vision of how our race was to be run, but I also needed people's ownership. So we discussed every element of the campaign in detail.

It was also vital to know each crew member's agenda. I am competitive, but I could only compete through my crew. If they do not give their best, the whole team will suffer. So what were each person's goals? One guy wanted to win at all costs. Another guy wanted simply to make it around the world. The key was to avoid agreeing to the lowest common denominator. So I said to the guy who just wanted to have an adventure, "You aren't competitive in your sailing, but you're certainly competitive in your work life. And I think you'll enjoy the race more if we're sailing fast and if we're doing things professionally." But I also had to be realistic, setting a goal like 'win the race' just isn't credible. So I said to the 'all-or-nothing' guy: "To finish first, first we have to finish. We have to sail smart. If we go for broke, sooner or later we'll blow up." After much discussion, the team worked out a statement of strategic intent:

"To build a campaign capable of winning the Global Challenge"

The words were chosen carefully. "To build a campaign" meant that the work started NOW, nine months before the race. The phase "that is capable of winning" meant the planning and preparation was devoted to one goal – to make the boat go faster. Driven by a passion we all felt, each individual personally committed themselves to striving to put 'Toshiba' in the top 3 of every leg. Our often repeated values as a crew were simple: Safe, Happy and Fast.

Professionalism was crucial – because we were literally dealing with matters of life and death. From the outset I insisted on high standards in everything we did and the crew responded superbly. Time keeping was impeccable; the yacht was cleaned and cleaned again. We took great pride in our crew uniform and kit. The BT Global Challenge is a race for amateurs – in the sense that the crew are unpaid – but the level of professionalism and commitment to the race by the crew was humbling. It was a joy to lead them. No one was ever late for a watch

– not ever. This is important. If you can't trust your team mate to turn up on time, can you trust him or her with your life?

The joy of yacht racing is that it stretches you in so many ways – particularly in the area of problem-solving. The BT Global Challenge consists of yachts with the same design. So it is incredibly difficult to sail your yacht faster than the other crews. But you can gain competitive advantage when things go wrong – as they surely they will in 30,000 miles of racing. So we spent time: a) Anticipating potential problems; b) Planning how to tackle the unexpected as quickly and efficiently as possible. The crew demonstrated a fantastic level of creativity and ingenuity. Dealing with the unexpected, we prided ourselves on getting a temporary solution up and running as soon as possible, thus minimising the effect on our performance. We then concentrated on a permanent solution. Minimising down-time was a key element to success.

Everybody's commitment was crucial. Sailing in the depths of the Southern Ocean, for example, it was icy cold, windy, wet and exhausting. The people who had finished their watch would go below to snatch some sleep. After 30 minutes spent getting out of soaking kit, they would slide into their mouldy, damp sleeping bag, and it took another 30 minutes to reverse the process. People therefore only had 3 hours of the 4 hour 'off-watch' available for sleep. The crew always slept on the high side of the yacht – which optimised the balance and made it sail faster. When we needed to tack – change direction – the 'off-watch' crew would get up and take their sleeping bag to the other side. Such a change-over might happen 2 or 3 times during their 3 hours rest. Not a single person complained and the entire crew did this day after day across the Southern Ocean. No leader on Earth could make 13 other exhausted people do this UNLESS they had all bought in into the idea. Everyone was committed.

So did we achieve peak performance? Of the 7 races we sailed on Toshiba (6 legs and the qualifying race) we finished in the top 3 on every occasion but one. Whilst we came 2nd in the 10 month long Global Challenge, one comment made by Geoff, a crew member, as we approached the finish line in Southampton meant a huge amount to me. "Second is not bad for the first lap - we will do better on the second!" I truly believe that he and the rest of the team would do it again. It struck me that we had built something to last.

On Day One we had identified the race as a learning race. The crew that could pass on knowledge amongst each other faster than others would certainly be hard to beat. On the first leg, I was available virtually every hour of every day – coaching, guiding and instructing as well as making decisions and technical calls. At that time, I joked that I wanted to spend the last leg in bed! But the fruits of the early learning certainly paid dividends.

Arriving in Boston 7 months later, we entered a complicated and unknown harbour, populated by rocks, channels and shipping traffic. With a spinnaker flying which required gibing – a difficult manoeuvre, changing from one side to the next – we weaved our way into the harbour. We also had to change the spinnaker for a smaller 'reaching' spinnaker during one short section of our approach. A crew member needed to go to the end of the spinnaker pole – 5 metres over the side of the yacht. We then hoisted a new spinnaker inside the old one, so that we could then take the old one down. This is known as a "peel", a tricky operation when each sail is bigger than a tennis court. The crew did this flawlessly twice during the approach as the many spectator boats and news helicopter watched. What did I do during the whole hour or so it took? Nothing – apart from wandering around the yacht with a cup of tea and a camera. We were well-up in the learning race!

So did we build a super team? In my eyes, of course, we did. But there were clearly things we could have done better. I still have a huge satisfaction for what we achieved on "Toshiba". The key part was getting buy-in to the agreed goals and at the end of the race we had all 'grown'. There are many stories and people have gone to greater things in sailing – but mostly people have used it as a springboard in 'life'. They have used the self knowledge to give them a confidence and perspective which is hard to match. And looking back, what were the 'take away' lessons? One above all: Enjoy it. Otherwise you have missed the point, which is probably the same rule in life.

c) *You can clarify your special contribution*

You can combine your strengths and successful style to clarify your special contribution. If you want to get paid, however, it is vital to identify the specific results you can deliver to a sponsor. Alison Fulford married her ability to deliver great service, for example, with leading high impact projects that benefited organisations. Today many savvy people are learning to balance their soul work and salary work.

People who take this step are more likely to follow their vocation. Your vocation is your calling – it is what you are here to do – and may be expressed in a recurring life-theme. The 'red thread' in your life may be, for example: helping people to develop their talents; solving problems; making the world a better place or whatever. Your vocation remains constant. Over the years, however, you will employ different vehicles for expressing it on the road towards doing valuable work. And you never retire from your vocation.

Jacqui Smith followed her vocation. Several years ago she attended a career management workshop I ran for people who wanted to make a living doing what they loved. (Jacqui's story was described in *The Class Act Book* – but the following pages bring it up-to-date in the piece called *HomeSmiths*.) Looking back at the satisfying projects in her life, she found a recurring theme was 'creating enriching environments'. She decided to pool her talents with David, her husband, a superb carpenter. They now specialise in providing interior design, bespoke furniture and enriching environments for customers. Coming from a sales background, she was able to translate the *HomeSmiths*' offering into benefits that appealed to customers. Beginning by working for family and friends, Jacqui and David found customers through their network. They are doing work they love and have built a thriving business.

'HomeSmiths'

Jacqui Smith

As a child I could spend hours creating room sets for my dolls, fiddling with doll's house furniture, making camps for my brother to play in or rearranging my bedroom. Whilst I followed art and excelled at it through my childhood and teens, my school was fiercely academic. So when it came to 'A' Level choices, Art was dropped in favour of Economics, Maths and German! University followed and I gained a degree in Economics and Maths. Having little clue of what I wanted to do, I found myself in sales and marketing, which is where I stayed for some years.

Feeling unfulfilled with my work, job changes ensued but I was never really addressing the root problem. Sales and marketing were not playing to my strengths. This left a whole host of skills and, more importantly, passions untapped. Outside work I was continuing with more creative pursuits, such as designing room schemes for myself as well as friends and family. But I never thought of doing this for a living, telling myself: "I'm not trained in Interior Design – how could I make money from this and why would anyone take me seriously?" Despite constant encouragement from friends, I remained unhappy in the corporate world.

Several years ago I went on a two day workshop aimed at helping people to make a living doing what they loved. Focusing on my passions, talents, dreams and goals threw up a common theme which simply read as 'creating enriching environments'. I then met my now husband David, a cabinet maker. He had always wanted to run his own business – yet possessed none of the required sales, marketing or organisational skills. Within months of meeting, we were engaged. We also knew then that we would one day set up on our own. David continued to design and make furniture in the short to medium term. In the longer term, however, he wanted to get more involved in bigger interior design projects. I wanted to help people enrich their living environments with colour and texture – plus take on the challenge of running a business. A brainstorm and a bottle of wine later 'HomeSmiths' was born. The name really says it all – the

Smiths with designs on your home! It also offers us so much flexibility in terms of what we offer our clients and will enable us to adapt and change the focus of an interior design based business in the future without worrying about the relevance of the brand we have created.

The response from our immediate network was tremendous. Not only did people believe in the proposition, but truly believed in David's and my ability, through our combined talents, to deliver. Starting the business when our first son Cameron was 4 months old, people thought we were mad – but staying in our old roles was so much more frightening!

It has been hard work and almost five years on we are still of course a young business, but we are constantly building our reputation. Our second son Piers was born two years ago and whilst the order book was full on the day of his arrival, the fact that my eye was quite understandably off the marketing ball for a few months did impact the business for a little while.

We have people telling us that we are lucky but I really don't think it's about luck. To me, self employment is a constant challenge; a challenge that I am more than happy to face, but we're kept on our toes constantly. Overcoming the tests we face brings with it that enormous sense of achievement and I suppose pride in what we have built together. Going outside my comfort zone is a regular occurrence; I don't think that you can build and develop a business without forcing yourself into uncharted waters! I go outside my comfort zone and then as soon as I return to that state of ease and confidence, I see that I have to expand the zone again!

We have had to be open to opportunities and never look at them on face value. The best example of this was in our first year of trading when I wrote to a local business, introducing HomeSmiths. A couple of follow up calls produced nothing until six months later the phone rang. For once 'we'll put your letter on file' meant just that and they were calling to ask us to quote for some boardroom furniture. The person calling was Elaine Erskine who is now one of my closest friends, God Mother to Piers and more importantly from a networking point of view has not only given us business herself but introduced us to five new customers.

As a team, we work together incredibly well. Some projects involve both of us; David focusing on the furniture with me designing the overall room scheme; other projects see us working independently. As far as the running of the business is concerned, we play to our strengths; David focuses on the designing and making whilst I manage the books and oversee the sales and marketing.

We pride ourselves on our quality of product and service. Although bespoke furniture is not exactly a regular purchase, we have now developed a loyal client base where people come back to us for more work and recommend us to friends. One lesson I learned on the workshop was to network but, most of all, to give something back to people in your network. So true and such a simple and cost effective way to grow a business! I am evangelical about doing work you love. And as a mother I will certainly encourage my children to follow their natural paths in life and work.

Jimmie Hepburn also follows his vocation – which is showing people how to build a more sustainable planet. As the Managing Director of Aquavision, he was a prime mover in developing the UK's first standard for aquaculture. You can read how he made this happen in the piece called *Aquavision: Bringing People Together to Achieve Positive Results.* The company provides a portfolio of services – from designing eco-friendly garden ponds to organic fish farming. (I met him when he created a pond for our garden.) Having run his own business for many years, Jimmie is street wise, yet also quite 'spiritual'. Believing people can learn valuable lessons from nature, he invites diverse groups to work together at the company's organic fish farm in Devon. How did he become interested in water? Jimmie writes:

"My father had a tropical fish tank. When I was five-years-old the fish had babies. This fascinated me and I went round the village telling people we had babies. Looking back, I always had an interest in nurturing living things and was interested in wildlife and the natural world. Conservation was coming to the fore at the beginning of the 70s so, instead of applying to study botany at university, I opted for one of the two courses available on Ecology. Field trips took me to Africa and Nepal. When studying rhinos and tigers, it dawned on me conserving that natural habitat was the key to helping animals to survive and thrive. Vast areas of natural forest and grasslands in Nepal were being cleared to make room for the rapidly rising population as a result of a malaria eradication programme.

"I recall having a talk with a conservation officer in Nepal who told me that cutting down forest to satisfy the need for agricultural land was not a long term solution. He said that before long more demands would be made for more forest to be cut as development meant a rise in population, and a rise in population meant more land was needed to feed that population. This and other similar examples I came across during my work sowed the seed for me to look at the human dimension in ecology."

"After leaving university I joined a fish farming company. There I rose from the hatchery to being General Manager and employing 50 people. The main product was salmon. Eventually we had to downsize and become more efficient. So I left and went to Germany to deepen my knowledge of organic fish farming. Inheriting a little money, I did a MSc. in human ecology, which was the answer to a prayer. My thesis was on how sustainability could work in Scottish Aquaculture: how we could meet our basic needs yet also develop sustainability. Organic farming could work and produce financial benefits for the fish farmers. After doing consultancy work at a fish farm, I started Aquavision in 1999. Penny, my partner, has been vital. She came from a family business, is good with figures and dreamed of us working together. So far, so good. We have paid the bills and built a business. We still create ponds for people and do consultancy – but are now also running our organic fish farm in Devon."

John Steinberg is another person who does valuable work. An American living in Sweden, he has published over 30 books on education that have had a massive influence in schools and universities. During the 1970s he introduced Values Clarification into education across Scandinavia, providing many tools that students could use to find and follow their values in life. John has the ability to bring learning to life for students, enabling and empowering them to take charge of their futures. He continues to share his knowledge with teachers and students via keynote speeches, newsletters, workshops and a stream of inspiring books. John describes how he started on his journey in the piece called *Finding My Vocation.*

Aquavision: Bringing People Together to Achieve Positive Results

Jimmie Hepburn

I feel passionately about saving the planet through community. Because of the finite resources, our survival depends on human beings relating to each other in a consensual way. This means that people need to develop a new relationship with the planet. We can get what we need through working with – rather than against – nature. Nature has got it sussed. There is no such thing as an environmental problem. On both social and economic level, we need to mimic nature. Let me explain how this can be translated into practice. For example, in 1997 I helped to develop the UK's first organic standard for aquaculture. Here is how we made it happen.

Stage 1: Bringing people together

The draft standard for organic aquaculture, created in 1989, had made little impression, so I contacted the Technical Director of the Soil Association. Deciding to finally get something off the ground, we convened a meeting at Bristol University. The session brought together fish farmers, retailers, feed manufacturers, academics and the Soil Association. Our aim was to consider the feasibility of developing a workable set of organic standards in aquaculture. Many of the parties had never met before and, seeing the mutual benefits of cooperation, they decided to set-up a working party to explore issues concerned with developing an organic aquaculture standard in the UK.

Stage 2: Involving the wider community

The next stage was setting up a series of meetings around the UK. I contacted over 60 organisations and individuals that had shown a direct interest in this subject. A range of experts were invited along to each meeting which was covering a specific topic. A key object behind these meetings was for the Soil Association to get to know about fish farming etc and for the fish farming industry to learn about organic farming. This had never been done before in aquaculture and it was crucial prior to drawing up a new standard.

My role was to orchestrate the process. I provided the secretariat services, such as making contacts, organising meetings, writing minutes and formulating draft standards. My experience in fish faming and sustainable development – coupled with my passion to see something tangible emerge from the process – helped to ensure that the learning process was working. Keeping to a tight time schedule, we produced a draft set of standards for assessment by the Council of the Soil Association within 18 months. All work was voluntary.

Stage 3: Getting tangible results

The launch of the new standard was announced at the British Trout Association annual conference in 1998. The chairperson of the Soil Association, Helen Browning, gave an excellent speech to delegates on this new area of aquaculture. As the standard was approved more people became interested, so I could forsake my role. That released me to concentrate on the next bit of pioneering.

Looking back on the whole process, I learned several things, including

- *Be alert, act on intuition, be persistent and believe in what you are doing.*

- *Recognise that developing new ideas often needs cooperation. This means understanding the desires of the differing stakeholders. I learned to highlight common areas of interest which could lead to mutual benefits.*

- *It is possible to create an environment in which people can develop new relationships, share ideas and be respected. This is vital, because introducing and implementing new ideas needs people with sensitivity, courage and energy.*

- *Be realistic about implementation – especially if it involves many different groups. Plan your timetable, double it, then multiply it by five!*

Let's return to the beginning when I talked about what we can learn from nature. I like to bring together groups that would not normally meet – and – provide a platform for them to be able to see what they have in common. People can then connect and use their diverse talents to solve problems. This is what happened when we developed the UK's first organic standard for aquaculture – but I can give many other examples. For instance, I frequently bring together different groups to co-operate. I have been looking for a place where I could practice this on a larger scale and have now found one in Devon. Penny, my wife, and I will grow fish organically and also create small micro-aquaculture systems. We will bring together the experience in fish farming and creating ponds in gardens.

There also needs to be a community dimension. I have a picture of people coming – not just to visit, but to work. I love working outside, because I feel much closer to nature. If people could do this more, we would re-establish our connection with nature. People can come and learn how to grow their own fish in their back garden, like they do tomatoes. We can provide a laboratory for them to get this feeling and they will take it back home. That way we spread the philosophy across the planet.

Finding My Vocation

John Steinberg

On the airplane home for Thanksgiving I looked out and saw the city of Detroit below me. Amazing. There, exactly as my professor described it, was the city in circled layers – the industrial centre, the older city homes and then the suburbs with their new business districts and larger homes. The theory of the sociology lesson became a reality.

As I started to get interested in education, I read the books of Ivan Illich and Neil Postman questioning the legitimacy of school as an institution. And then it hit me. A new pattern was revealed. Thinking of my high school in Rochester, New York, suddenly I saw how the rooms and students were placed in physical order. The retarded children were placed in basement homerooms, the honours students in upper floor special classes. How strange. How unfair. How could I not see the pattern as a student at the school?

Jim Crowfoot – a native American professor of the psychology of religion, one of my favourite teachers at the University of Michigan, meets me on a street in Ann Arbor, Michigan and asks what I will do when I graduate. "I'm interested in education, but all the schools of education are so hopelessly boring, I've heard." "Try the University of Massachusetts". I never met Professor Crowfoot again, but I virtually ran to Amherst, Massachusetts from Ann Arbor.

What a feast for the eyes – special projects, displays and happenings all around. I must study there. After talking myself in, I enrolled in teacher training courses. BORING. Very Boring. Terrible. And I let them know it at a planning meeting as I, in my shy, but stubborn way I showed my disappointment. "Come with me to my office," said Dr Dwight Allen, Dean of the School of Education. "Now, what do you want to do?" "I want to work with dropouts, reform the public school system, start folk high schools after the Scandinavian model." He got on the phone. "Is this the administration office? Fine. This is Dr. Allen. Drop John Steinberg's programme and courses. I'll be his personal advisor for an independent study program." Dr Allen turned to me,

"Well, John, that's fixed. Now do your thing and report back to me." I was off and running.

School reform became dear to me, but soon the life theme of empowerment became my golden thread. How can students learn to help themselves? How can teachers feel more empowered to take charge of their own work situation? How can more people build their lives around their personal passions? How can I help my own three sons to verbalise and then realise their vision, while using their key strengths and talents?

The meaning of life, according to my definition, is to give others hope. That's it. If you have hope you are all the more likely to help yourself and to help others. Slowly but surely a pattern developed in my own professional life. I had a passion for empowerment and school reform. I had a purpose – to give teachers and students hope. I discovered two talents that were never discovered as I grew up. Writing and public speaking came very easily to me. I loved the applause and the laughter and I loved the structure I could give explaining complicated theories in an easy-to-understand form. "Here's an idea you can use and make your own in order to make a difference at your school or your workplace or your home."

I loved the writing. It wasn't hard at all. "Have something to say. Find a form. Say it simply and then stop." Moving to Sweden, I quickly found myself at a conference on developing social skills in schools. In my hesitant but eager American-Swedish I presented my ideas about values clarification, self-concept training and other methods I took with me from the University of Massachusetts. "Why, you should write a book about that," say Jan Heimer and Anna Lisa Melldén and here's a little money for it too. "That's not hard to do as long as I have something to say." And I was off running. 30 books later I am still running with the books, together with the public speaking, two ways to pass on knowledge. At the same time, writing and public speaking give me my flow and peaks.

There is no greater satisfaction than seeing an idea strike a chord in another person. I blast my audience with ideas, check lists and words of encouragement. I help them to find patterns and possibilities that others have helped me find. In the future I hope to do more one-to-

one sessions with young people helping to find their patterns of strength and talent. For instance, recently I met a 15-year-old boy who wants to be a doctor. "Fine. And that takes lots of perseverance. How have you shown perseverance up to now?" And together we discovered his pattern of perseverance from five years of almost daily football practice. His eyes lit up and he was one realisation closer to going for his vision.

Is there peace at the end of the rainbow? Probably not for me - I'm a "never 100% satisfied" kind of guy. Yet, people have helped me discover patterns and possibilities. I will continue to do that for others through my books and public speaking and more one-on-one mentoring. In the end, following the path of empowerment and giving others hope is surely a means to bring inner peace upon myself and peace upon the world.

Now let's tackle the crunch question. "So far many people you mention have been leaders or have gone solo," somebody may say. "Is it possible to play to your strengths and do satisfying work within an organisation?" The answer is "Yes," but with provisos. Think like a freelancer and follow three rules. First, clarify what you can offer to sponsors. Second, show how it will benefit the business. Third, find a good manager. Today enlightened organisations are encouraging people to use their talents. They are creating 'win-wins' for both the employee and employer. *But ultimately you will need to craft your perfect role.*

How to make this happen? Try tackling the exercise at the end of this chapter called *My Perfect Role.* This invites you to clarify your perfect project, people and place. Let's explore these steps.

1) Project

Describe the characteristics of the kind of 'project' you find stimulating. One person wrote, for example: 'Looking back at the satisfying projects in my life, I can identify several patterns. I love doing work that contributes to improving the quality of people's lives. At University, for example, I organised the first ever sponsored 'Fun Run', raising £10,000 for charity. Early on in my IT career, I launched software that enabled students to take charge of their own learning. The projects I enjoy also have a deadline, which is probably the way I work best." What are the characteristics of the projects you find fulfilling?

2) People

Describe the characteristics of the kind of people – both customers and colleagues – you find stimulating. The person wrote: "If I am working for a company, I must have a boss I respect. When leading a team, I must have positive team members who are prepared to work hard. The customers I like are those who are at the forefront of their field. They may be demanding, but they also make quick decisions." What kinds of people do you work with best?

3) Place

Describe the characteristics of the 'place' – the culture and environment – you find stimulating. The person wrote: "I like working in the 'newer' industries – such as IT and communications. They are professional, informal and are also making the rules for the future." Describe the kind of culture in which you feel at home.

Clarify what you can offer a potential sponsor. Bearing in mind your answers, describe: a) The perfect project you would like to tackle. b) The *specific results* you could deliver to a potential employer by delivering this project. c) The steps you can take to find or create such a project. Later we will look at how your soul work can also become your salary work.

It is time to move on. The following pages provide questions and exercises a person can use to identify their talents. The next chapter explores how to translate these strengths into specific goals.

Strengths:

Trigger Questions

The following pages provide trigger questions that a person can consider to clarify their strengths, successful style and special contribution.

a) *Strengths*

- What are your strengths? What are the activities in which you consistently deliver A's, rather than B's or C's?

- What are your passions? What do you feel passionately about? Which of these passions can you translate into a 'project' where you score at least an 8/10?

- What gives you positive energy? What are the activities in which you feel positively engaged, rather than partly or pretend engaged?

- When do you feel in your element? When do you feel ease and yet also able to excel? When do you feel calm, clear and deliver concrete results?

- When do you quickly see the destination – the picture of perfection? When do you go A, B...then jump to....Z? When do you see the big picture but also have attention to detail?

- Where do you quickly see patterns? Where do you have good 'personal radar'? Where do you have a 'memory of the future'?

- When do you go into your equivalent of the 'zone'? When do things go 'slowly but speedily'? What are the activities where you can make complicated things simple?

- What are the activities where you are a good finisher? What are those where you are naturally self-disciplined? What are those where you score highly on drive, detail and delivery?

- When do you flow, focus, finish and, as a by-product, gain fulfilment? What are the activities in which you enjoy the journey as much as reaching the goal?

- When do you follow your passion, translate it into a clear purpose, achieve peak performance and sometimes gain a sense of peace?

b) *Successful Style*

- Let's explore your successful style – the way you work best. Looking back on your life, describe what for you have been three satisfying 'projects'. Use the term 'project' in its broadest sense. For example: passing an exam, travelling around Europe, designing a web site, running a marathon, shipping a product, writing an article, leading a team or whatever.

- Looking at each project in turn, then do several things. First: Describe the example in detail. Second: Describe the specific things that made it satisfying. Finally, looking at each of these projects, can you see any patterns? Bearing in mind any patterns that have emerged, describe what you believe is your successful style.

c) *Special Contribution*

- Before moving onto your special contribution, let's look back at your successful style. Does this give any clues to your vocation?

- Your vocation is your calling – it is what you are here to do – and may be expressed in a recurring life-theme. The 'red thread' in your life may be, for example: helping people to develop their talents; solving problems; making the world a better place or whatever. Your vocation remains constant. Over the years, however, you will employ different vehicles for expressing it on the road towards doing valuable work. What do you think is your vocation?

- Let's move onto your special contribution. We need to consider how you might combine your strengths – what you do best – with your successful style – how you work best. Putting these things together, what do you think might be your special contribution? What might be your potential niche? What might be the special 'project' you would find fulfilling? If you had a blank piece of paper and could design your perfect role, would be it be?

- Let's consider how to turn this into something to offer to potential sponsors. We can explore three factors: the project, people and place.

  Project. Describe the characteristics of the kind of project you find stimulating.

  People. Describe the characteristics of the kind of people you find stimulating – both customers and colleagues.

  Place. Describe the characteristics of the 'place' – culture and environment – you find stimulating.

  Bearing your answers in mind, describe: a) The perfect 'project'; b) The specific results you could deliver to a potential employer by delivering this project; c) The steps you can take to find or create such a project.

Strengths

Exercises

The following pages provide exercises that a person can use to clarify their strengths.

My Strengths: The activities in which I consistently deliver A's

A's. The activities in which I deliver A's are when I am:

- ....

- ....

- ....

B's. The activities in which I deliver B's are when I am:

- ....

- ....

- ....

C's. The activities in which I deliver C's are when I am:

- ....

- ....

- ....

Building on my strengths

Bearing in mind my A talents, I believe my best contribution to an employer would be to:

● ....

....

The benefits an employer would get from me making this contribution would be to:

● ....

....

The steps I can therefore take to keep developing and using my 'A' talents are to:

● ....

....

The steps I can take to manage the consequences of my B's and C's are to:

● ....

....

My Passions: Translating some of these passions into a least an 8/10

**My passions – and the things
I feel passionately about – are:**

● ....

● ....

● ....

● ....

**The passions that I can translate into a
'project' where I score at least an 8/10 are:**

● ....

....

● ....

....

Positive Energy

The things that give me positive energy are when I am:

- ....

  ....

- ....

  ....

- ....

  ....

The steps I can take to do more of these things are to:

- ....

- ....

- ....

Positively Engaged

Positively Engaged. The situations in which I feel positively – and fully – engaged are when I am:

- ....

- ....

- ....

Partly Engaged. The situations in which I feel partly engaged are when I am:

- ....

Pretend Engaged. The situations in which I feel 'pretend' engaged are when I am:

- ....

Action Plan. Bearing these answers in mind, the steps I want to take are to:

- ....

My Element

**The activities in which I feel in my element
– at ease and yet able to excel – are when I am:**

- ....

  ....

- ....

  ....

- ....

  ....

**The things I can do to put myself
into more of these situations are to:**

- ....

- ....

- ....

Fulfilment

The activities I find most fulfilling are when I am:

- ....

....

- ....

....

- ....

....

**The steps I can take to do
more of these things are to:**

- ....

- ....

- ....

Calmness

The situations in which I am calm, clear and deliver concrete results are when I am:

- ....

  ....

- ....

  ....

- ....

  ....

The things I can do to put myself into more of these situations are to:

- ....

- ....

- ....

Flow

The times when I experience
a sense of flow are when I am:

- ....

....

- ....

....

- ....

....

The steps I can take to do
more of these things are to:

- ....

- ....

- ....

Enjoying The Journey

**The activities in which I enjoy the journey
as much as reaching the goal are when I am:**

- ....

  ....

- ....

  ....

- ....

  ....

**The steps I can take to do
more of these things are to:**

- ....

- ....

- ....

Seeing The Destination Quickly: Going A, B.................Z

The situation in which I go 'A, B.....Z' is when I am:

● ....

....

The things I then do right to deliver 'Z' are:

● ....

● ....

● ....

The things I can do to put myself into more situations where I deliver 'Z' are to:

● ....

● ....

● ....

Seeing Patterns

**The situations in which I can quickly
see patterns are when I am:**

- ....
....

- ....
....

- ....
....

**The things I can do to put myself
into more of these situations are to:**

- ....

- ....

- ....

Making Complicated Things Simple

**The activities in which I can make
complicated things simple are when I am:**

● ....

....

● ....

....

● ....

....

**The steps I can take to do
more of these activities are to:**

● ....

● ....

● ....

Delivery: The 3 D's

People who do brilliant work score highly on the 3 D's. This exercise invites you to rate yourself in these areas of Drive, Detail and Delivery. Make sure you score a total of at least 24/10.

The Activity In Which I Want To Do Superb Work Is:

- ....

- **Drive**
  The extent to which I have a strong drive and desire to do this activity is:

  .../10

- **Detail**
  The extent to which I have attention to detail when doing this activity is:

  .../10

- **Delivery**
  The extent to which I deliver the goods when doing this activity is:

  .../10

My Successful Style

This exercise invites you to identify your successful style – the way you work best. Start by describing what for you have been three satisfying 'projects'. Use the term 'project' in its widest sense. First: Describe the example in detail. Second: Describe the specific things that made it satisfying. Finally, looking at each of these projects, can you see any patterns? Bearing in mind any patterns that have emerged, clarify what you believe is your successful style. Finally, describe the things you can do to try to follow your successful style in the future.

My Satisfying Projects: FIRST Example

The satisfying project was when I:

* ....

The specific things that made it satisfying were:

* ....

* ....

* ....

My Satisfying Projects: SECOND Example

The satisfying project was when I:

● ....

The specific things that made it satisfying were:

● ....

● ....

● ....

My Satisfying Projects: THIRD Example

The satisfying project was when I:

● ....

The specific things that made it satisfying were:

● ....

● ....

● ....

My Successful Style

Bearing in mind any patterns that have emerged, describe what you believe to be your successful style. (You may, of course, have several different successful styles. For example: One when working alone; another when working with other people.)

My successful style is that I work best when:

- I..

- I..

- I..

- I..

My Successful Style: Following It In The Future

The things I can do to try to follow
my successful style in the future are to:

- ....

- ....

- ....

My Perfect Role:
The 'Project', People & Place

Project. The kind of project I find stimulating is one where I am able to:

- ....

....

....

People. The kinds of people – colleagues and customers – I find stimulating are those who are

- ....

- ....

- ....

Place. The kind of place – culture and environment – I finding stimulating is one which is:

- ....

....

My Perfect Role.
Finding or creating it

**Bearing these answers in mind,
my perfect 'project' would be to:**

● ....

   ....

**The specific results I could deliver to an
employer by doing this project would be to:**

● ....

● ....

● ....

**The steps I can take to find or
create such a project are to:**

● ....

● ....

● ....

My Vocation

Vocation I believe my vocation is to:

- ....

  ....

**Vehicles. The different vehicles I
can use to express my vocation are:**

- ....

- ....

- ....

**Valuable Work. The specific ways I can
translate this into doing valuable work are to:**

- ....

- ....

- ....

My Special Contribution

My Strengths. My strengths –
what I do best – are that I am able to:

● ....

....

My Successful Style. My
successful style – how I work best – is to:

● ....

....

My Special Contribution. Putting together my
strengths and successful style, I believe my
best contribution to an employer would be to:

● ....

The benefits that this contribution could
deliver to a potential employer would be to:

● ....

STEP 2:

SPECIFIC GOALS

Everybody can set specific goals. People have always wanted to follow their dreams – and this often involves pursuing the peak performer's path. (See illustration.) They start by doing something they feel passionately about – then translate this into a clear purpose. Sometimes this means pursuing an odyssey. They may aim to discover a medical cure, turn-around a business or achieve a personal Holy Grail. This may involve an outer journey, an inner journey or a combination of both. They are super professional, solve problems and achieve peak performance. Some also pass on their knowledge to future generations. People who achieve their goal enjoy a sense of peace – if only for a short time. They then embark again upon the peak performer's path.

Bengt Elmen has translated his strengths into specific goals. Suffering severe injuries at birth when oxygen failed to reach his brain, he needs ongoing assistance to dress, move and eat. He has a mischievous sense of humour, however, and is a brilliant lecturer and business person. Overcoming setbacks, he graduated from university and built a £20 million company helping disabled citizens to improve their quality of life. He created another business giving keynote speeches showing how people can take responsibility for shaping their future. Bengt believes in 'controlling the controllables'. He builds on what he can control, rather than worries about what he can't control. He describes his approach in the piece called *Decide Your Destiny*.

"I love working with Achievers. Such people are prepared to take responsibility and build on what they have got. Deciding what they want to do, they then work hard to achieve their dreams. People do not define the hand of cards they are given at birth, but they do decide how to use the cards. That is what I mean by *Decide Your Destiny*."

The Peak Performer's Path

*They have a positive attitude
and pursue the following steps:*

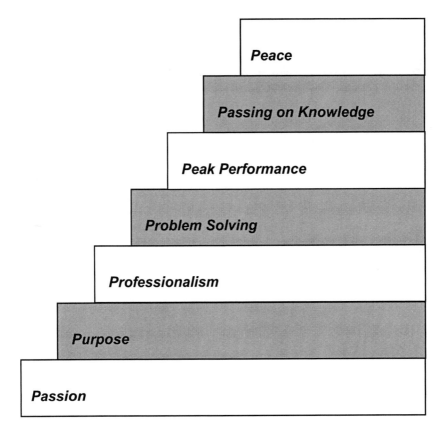

Bengt lectures across the world. Audiences watch him arrive on stage and sit respectfully – waiting to learn from a person who has obviously overcome adversity. They came to listen to a 'guest speaker', but soon realise they may learn about themselves. Bengt specialises in positive reframing. He says: "I type books by using an instrument strapped to my forehead. Yes, it takes longer to type. But it actually gives me more time to think when I am writing." Bengt takes people on a psychological journey. His messages are: "Take responsibility. Build on your strengths. Be an achiever." People in the audience begin to focus on their dreams – and plan how to turn these into reality.

So how can you clarify your picture of perfection? If you wish, you can focus on three themes: a) You can set specific goals; b) You can, if appropriate, find potential sponsors (a sponsor is somebody who may hire you for doing what you do best); c) You can clarify your strategy for achieving the specific goals. Let's explore these steps.

Decide Your Destiny

Bengt Elmèn

'Survivor' speeches have become very popular at conferences over the last few years. People who invite me to speak have often heard how previous audiences began to see things in perspective. I use humour to show how I coped with my 'tragic fate', explaining that it is possible to see hardships from two perspectives: positive or negative. People often leave the session finding it harder to complain about trivialities, such as the food being too cold when they go home at night. The sessions show it is possible to overcome great difficulties, rather than drown in depression. This is a message of hope and joy – and people are forced to re-examine challenging situations in their own lives. But I have a confession to make. I am not interested in giving 'Survivor' speeches anymore. Why? I am more interested in giving 'Achiever' speeches.

I love working with Achievers. Such people are prepared to take responsibility and build on what they have got. Deciding what they want to do, they then work hard to achieve their dreams. People do not define the hand of cards they are given at birth, but they do decide how to use the cards. That is what I mean by 'Decide Your Destiny'. Whether giving keynotes or facilitating mentoring sessions, I focus on three key messages with people.

1) Take Responsibility

Achievers are prepared to take responsibility for their lives. Perhaps that is why I like working with them. As far as I know, this is the only life I have got. I met death already at birth due to lack of oxygen, but I disregarded him. I chose life. Since then death has been a reality to me. Life is short and it's no use hiding from the fact that we all are going to die some day. Therefore I want to be in charge of my own life. I want to decide how I spend the time that has been given to me. I don't want to leave that to anyone else. It is my responsibility and I am not ready to spoil a second. My first book in Swedish, 'Your responsibility and Mine', provoked quite a response. Why? Because I was urging people to do what they could do, rather than complain about what they couldn't do. This links to my second message.

2) *Build On What You Have Got*

Did Stevie Wonder stop singing because of his lack of sight? What about José Feliciano, Ray Charles and Andrea Bocelli? Did Stephen Hawking shape his life based on his doctors' early death sentences? Did Helen Keller's difficulties stop her helping other people? Did Franklin D Roosevelt refuse to carry-out the Presidency because he suffered from Polio? If Ludwig van Beethoven had focused on what he lacked – rather than what he had - we would not have heard his Ninth Symphony and its tribute to the joy of life.

Life has taught me to build on what I have got. My physical abilities do not always reach 10/10! My walking ability is probably 3/10. But I decided to transport myself from the physical world to the mental world – so I became fascinated by people's hopes, ideas, plans and ambitions. I manage the physical world with the help of technical aids and my personal assistants. For example, let me explain how I write. Right now that I am hitting each key on my Mac with a stick that is fastened to a band around my head. It is not the fastest way in the world, but it gives me time to think about what I want to write. (Think different!) While other authors use their hands at work, I use my head. (And heart.) So that is how you turn a limitation into a strength. That is how you build on what you have got.

And when you have chosen to concentrate on what you have got, then you also have to pick the direction of your life. This brings us to my third message.

3) *Dare To Be An Achiever – But Do It Your Way*

Achievers have a special quality. They decide what they want to do – then they do it. Perhaps all of us have listened to inspiring keynote speakers who urged us to follow our dreams. But then what happens? The instant motivation begins to fade away and we return to our daily lives. If you look back at the times you have achieved, however, it is because: a) You made an inner decision to do something; b) You were prepared to work hard; c) You did it in your own way.

Pursuing your route can be affirming yet also lonely. In order to achieve greatness, you have to discover your own path.

Unfortunately, greatness never can be accomplished by copying someone else – and sometimes it means paying less attention to what others think. You will find it more beneficial to listen to your own inner voice when making the most important decisions in your life. Ask yourself: "What are my inner-most aspirations? What do I really want? What do I lack in my life right now? What do I want to accomplish within this lifetime?"

Creating new rules in the world can be difficult - but fun. I like to challenge people's traditional views of how life should be. Travelling around the world giving speeches, I found it interesting to try new ideas when I came home to Sweden. Once a taxi-driver picked me up at Stockholm airport and asked me where I had flown from. I answered: "America". So during the rest of the journey he treated me as an honoured guest and asked lots of intelligent questions in English, which I had great fun answering. He treated me very differently than if I had been perceived as a 'disabled Swede' who was returning home. Reaching my front door, he was rather shocked when I ended the conversation in Swedish.

Can the future be rainbow coloured – rather than grey? Speaking to people in the business world, the best response has always been from 'new' business people. They are unconventional, enjoy being challenged and want to discover new ways of looking at the world. The world of grey suits and grey ties finds it harder to take the messages on-board. (I'm too odd for them. My Manchester jeans do not fit-in.) The new business achievers, however, are going beyond old preconceptions. Just like the blind, deaf or disabled people I mentioned, some are prepared to follow their hearts and do what they are here to do.

My passion is to help achievers to find their purpose, possibilities and peace in life. Why? They love freedom – the freedom to be, the freedom to create – and so do I. Sometimes we all need somebody to say: "You can do it - let's explore how." My work is about helping people to make that decision - then putting it into practice. Inspirational speeches can be a start, but then comes the sweat. People are more willing to do the hard work, however, if they have taken the responsibility to decide their destiny.

a) You can set specific goals

People have different pictures of success. So let's begin by clarifying your picture. Try tackling the later exercise called *Success.* Imagine that you are looking back on your life when you are 80. Describe the things you will have done that for you will mean your life has been successful.

Success

Looking back on my life when I am 80, I will feel my life has been successful if I have done the following things:

● ....

● ....

● ....

People often answer this question by focusing on three themes.

Positive Relationships

They say things like: "I want to have given my children a happy childhood and a great start in life...to have been a good husband/wife...to have been a good friend."

Positive Difference

They say things like: "I want to have made a positive difference in the world." This leads to discussions about their vocation, which leads to statements like: "I want to have finished the book I have been promising to write....to have been a great teacher...to have created a different kind of company."

Positive Experiences

They say things like: "I want to have lived life fully...to have travelled the world...to have used my talents...to have no regrets."

Clarifying this long-term picture can provide you with an inner compass. Faced by a crucial decision, you can ask yourself: "Does taking this step contribute towards achieving my long term goals?" If the answer is "Yes," then fine. If not, then maybe it should be reconsidered.

Kajsa Berglind has always had a long-term picture of success. I met her in 1980 when she was 19. She had travelled 900 miles from her home in Kiruna, in the Arctic Circle, to attend a Personal Strength Building course near Stockholm. Kajsa stood out in the group of 32 people, many over twice her age. As befitted a member of a motor-bike gang, she was feisty, but also caring. Tackling the exercise called *My Ideal Life,* she described the future she wanted – full of children, animals and exciting projects. Kajsa went on to write books, run companies and inspire people across Sweden. She describes one of her latest projects in the piece called *Satra Brunn – Revitalising a 300 year-old Health Spa.*

Revitalising Satra Brunn – A 300 year-old Health Spa

Kajsa Berglind

Satra Brunn is a magical place that has regained its former glory. Four years ago it faced extinction. Now it is making a profit, attracts 25,000 visitors a year and turns over £3million. It has 110 buildings, dating from the 1700's, a health spa, a conference centre and a hotel. But first, let's go back four years.

– – – – – – – –

"The idea came when we were sitting at the kitchen table," has become a bit of a cliché, but in this case it is true. Since my early 20s I had combined building businesses with raising a family. In 2002 I was 39 and had spent the last few years caring for my fourth child, Maja. Looking back, I realised that I needed the years to care for my family and gather energy, but now I was a bit bored and longed to find my next 'heart project'. On that April day I was talking with Anders Ahlberg, who wanted help in starting his own business. After sorting out his plan, he looked me in the eye and said: "So what should we do about Satra Brunn?"

My heart jumped. Satra Brunn is a famous old health spa, located just 8 km from where I live near Sala. The place was bankrupt for the second time in just a few years. Since the University of Uppsala gave up its ownership of 'SB', the place had struggled. The estate of 114 wooden houses from the 18th Century onwards – plus 60 acres of lovely land – was under threat of being sold off separately. No single buyer wanted to purchase it from the lawyer handling the insolvency – so a piece of history was going to be broken-up. Could I do something by myself? No. But perhaps I could mobilise a group of people to revitalise the spa. "I think we should try to do something," I said to Anders. So we literally began planning there and then.

The Vision

Many years ago I learned about my strengths – plus the areas where I am not so strong! So I know what I can offer and which people I need around me to compensate for my weaknesses. Walking into an old ruined house, I immediately say: "Wow – this could be a palace." I see the finished article, children playing, people eating and the house living. Very quickly I had a clear vision for Satra Brunn. I am a strange mixture – having a big vision, but also an eye for detail. Satra Brunn could live again – it would be vital, exciting and profitable – but we also needed to get the money! The obstacles spurred me on – this was going to be hard work but fun.

We needed a task force – but a caring one. Satra Brunn has always stood for healing, so it must be rebuilt by caring people. Anders and I contacted a friend – then together we brainstormed the people we wanted to invite into the project. We needed people with certain characteristics, skills and access to networks. Honouring Satra Brunn's tradition of being a place of healing was crucial – but we also needed some people who knew how to run good businesses in the 21st Century.

Two months later we had gathered a committed team of 15 people. We agreed on the future vision for Satra Brunn. But that was the easy part. Anders and I became immersed in the joys of business plans, budgets, developing the legal platform for creating the business – a cooperative – and getting money from the banks. We placed a bid with the bankruptcy lawyer – and bought Satra Brunn for £300k. Going back to the bank, we borrowed another £150k for capital needs – and prayed it would last. Suddenly we found ourselves owning this enormous place, its obligations to its 30 employees and an empty booking system!

Pursuing The Vision

The work began. During the first 2 months I managed the company before we appointed a managing director. Then I took over the financial work – doing the book keeping and paying the salaries, throwing myself into sales, administration and taking care of the reception. Satra Brunn had to be recreated anew. Previously it had been pitched at the 'rehabilitation' market – one that no longer existed. So we had to find new customers. Building on the spa heritage, we aimed to create a hotel, restaurant and conference centre. The initial team of 15 volunteers grew in size, but that team worked without payment as part of their commitment to the project. We did, of course, pay the previous employees who remained – and slowly began to hire more paid staff.

The first 12 months were difficult. The MD we hired left and we also lost money. So we sold off one of the houses to balance the books. During the early weeks I spent a lot of time at Satra Brunn – walking in the parks, listening to the place and feeling the inspiration. Looking back, we had to make some tough decisions. Satra Brunn had a tradition of caring for patients who came for rehabilitation. Shifting to providing a new kind of service proved difficult. Some employees stayed on – and contracts needed to be honoured – but we needed to begin with a blank piece of paper. New staff were hired and some others were offered work as freelancers. As we have grown, every staff member who wanted to continue working in the new ethos has been offered a job and is back working with us. Some left by their own choice and that is fine.

Slowly the turnaround began to have an effect. Guest numbers increased and we got good coverage in the media. Income went up and we kept the costs to a minimum. We found a new managing director. She is a super professional who is used to working in bigger companies. She also liked and supported our values and way of doing business. Most of the original group are entrepreneurs who are used to running small businesses. Her approach made a huge difference. We quickly moved from fire fighting to planning ahead, creating a structure and delivering professional service to the guests.

Realising The Vision

Today Satra Brunn is thriving. The money has come in and we are in the black. My initial budget has actually proved to be quite realistic, even though we had no access to any historic figures. Everybody said we needed at least £1 million to get through the first year. After selling one of the houses for £100k, however, we managed to survive. Now we are embarking on getting more capital to continue converting the energy system from electricity to biofuel. Traditional banks are not interested, so we borrow from JAK Bank that provides interest free loans. The business keeps improving.

Last week we had a pub evening – an event we have held every Wednesday each summer for the past 4 years. The very first evening we had 7 people – last week we had 600. People were laughing, chatting and enjoying life. We are doing business with heart – and following the three key words that we agreed on when we started – Healing Learning and Creating. Most of all, we have revitalised Satra Brunn – a place that people have visited to feel good for over 300 hundred years. That is a tremendous legacy.

Kajsa embodies the paradoxes demonstrated by many peak performers. She is loving but tough – especially when people step over a certain moral line. Energetic and inspiring, she thrives on painting pictures of the future, yet also loves doing the accounts! She is spiritual, but creates systems that sustain businesses. Like many fine leaders, she combines the elements of being an Energiser, Educator and Enforcer:

- **Energisers:** they provide an inspiring vision, communicate a clear strategy and show people the road map for achieving the picture of perfection.

- **Educators:** they provide an encouraging environment and enable people to become self-managing, execute the strategy and achieve the picture of perfection.

- **Enforcers:** they provide the compass – the code of conduct – and are prepared to enforce the Dos and Don'ts if people do not follow the guidelines for achieving the picture of perfection.

Good leaders balance all three. Energy provides inspiration, but education is necessary to enable self-managing people to do superb work. Enforcement comes from providing a moral compass that everybody wants to implement. People see how following certain guidelines will help them to achieve success. Old style leaders sometimes relied on autocratic enforcement without, providing education. They ended up chasing their own tails, complaining about the quality of staff. Kajsa is a leader who embraces all three qualities and helps to build self-sustaining teams. She also took the next step, which is vital if people are to achieve positive results.

You can focus

'Focus' is a much used word and a bit of a cliché. Sometimes it is important to 'Spring Clean' our lives, however, and refocus on the things that are important. Clutter absorbs energy in both our personal and professional lives. Try tackling the later exercise called *The*

White Room. Imagine your life is an empty White Room. There is nothing in it except your family. You are then invited to do the following things.

1) *Put 3 people in your white room*

"Straight away I would put in my best friend and two other people – because they always give me positive energy," said one person. "Certainly I know many acquaintances – but few real kindred spirits. On the other hand, there are hundreds in my address book who I will never contact again. Perhaps I should spend more time with the people who really matter to me." Who would you put in your room?

2) *Put 3 strengths and 3 goals into your white room*

Ask yourself: "What are the 3 things I do best? Put your top 3 strengths into the room. Then clarify your goals. Linking back to the previous exercise on success, asked yourself: "What is my picture of success? What are my personal and professional goals?" Put your top 3 goals into the room.

3) *Put 3 possessions and 3 other things into your white room.*

Time for the treats. List the 3 possessions you want to put into the room. "My computer, television and CD player," said one person, before worrying about their running shoes, pets and mobile phone. Eventually they squeezed these into the '3 other things'. So what possessions would you put in the room? Plus what would be the 3 other things? So now you have your family plus 15 items – people, strengths, goals, possessions, other things – in your White Room.

Sounds drastic? Perhaps, but sometimes we need to spring-clean our lives. We can then concentrate on the people and activities that give us positive energy. Don't worry. Clutter will soon appear – and then it will be time for a new spring-clean.

Let's move on to doing fulfilling work. Sometimes you will work as an individual contributor, sometimes as a team member, sometimes as a leader. Let's explore your options.

You can clarify the possible roads you can travel – then set specific goals

Let's return to explore your work possibilities. Looking ahead to the future, what are the different roads you can travel? If you work in an organisation, for example, the obvious choices may be that you can: a) Stay in your present role; b) Try to expand the role to play to your strengths; c) Get another role inside the organisation; d) Move to another organisation; e) Go freelance; f) Do something completely different. Try tackling the exercise at the end of this chapter called *My Possible Options.* This invites you to take the following steps.

- Make a map of the possible routes you can take in the next couple of years. Describe the pluses and minuses of each option. Rate the attractiveness of each option. Do this on a scale 0 – 10.

- Be creative and consider other routes. For example: Is it possible to combine the best parts of each road into a new option?

- Bearing in mind your strengths and long-term picture of success, clarify the route you want to travel.

Take time to reflect before committing yourself to pursing a particular route. Return to your inner compass and ask yourself.

"Which route do I want to pursue? What will be the pluses? What will be the minuses? How can I build on the pluses and minimise the minuses? Am I prepared to accept the whole package? Will pursuing this route play to my strengths? How can I shape it so that I have even more opportunity to play to my strengths? Bearing in mind my strengths, how can I translate these into specific goals? For example, can I write an article, launch a product, lead a team or whatever? Will pursuing this route – and reaching the specific goal – contribute towards achieving my long-term picture of success?

Imagine you want to earn your living doing what you love. That will call for finding sponsors – people who will pay you for doing what you do best. Let's explore how to make this happen.

b) You can, if appropriate, find sponsors

Everybody understands that we are all self-employed now. (At least, I hope they do.) There are no lifetime jobs anymore, there are only projects. Even if you are 'employed' in a company, your job can vanish overnight. There are three routes people can take in their professional lives. These are: The Fulfilling Road, The Faustian Road and The Fulfilling Road + Finding Funding. Let's explore these routes.

1) The Fulfilling Road

People can do fulfilling work. They can pursue their passion – be it encouraging people, computing, the arts, teaching, architecture or whatever. Doing what they enjoy, they are not too concerned about money – providing they have enough to live on. The fulfilling road is pursued by many peak performers early-on in their working lives.

2) The Faustian Road

People can sell their soul for money and status – hoping that one day they will be free to do what they really want. If a person sells their soul, however, they may find it hard to reclaim their life and enjoy the anticipated rainbows. Some in the 'lucky generation' of high-tech employees gained enough money to get the choices they wished – but some got stuck in corporate no-man's land. Taking a fresh look at their lives, some then embarked on the next route.

3) The Fulfilling Road + Finding Funding

People learn how to do fulfilling work yet also get funding. They balance their soul-work and salary work, their mission and mortgage. Being both soul-wise and street-wise, they reach out to find potential sponsors – people who will hire them for doing what they do best. They then use their strengths to help the sponsors to succeed.

Fiona Strange chose to make a living doing what she loved. You can read her story in the piece called *Choosing To Follow My Dream.* She was doing temporary work at Microsoft while – taking a break from her studies to be a vet – when we met. Fiona loved animals and had been captivated by the TV series *All Creatures Great and Small.* She set her heart on being a vet, but now faced a dilemma because she also liked business. Should she continue with her studies? Qualification remained uncertain and, even if she qualified, she must compete to find work in a practice. Working in business would probably bring in more cash. Which route did she want to follow?

Fiona tackled the exercise called *My Possible Options.* (See end of this chapter.) She began by drawing the possible roads she could follow in the future – become a vet, go into business, combine the two or whatever. She also described the pluses and minuses of each option. Looking at the different routes, Fiona then rated the 'attractiveness' of each one on a scale 0 – 10. "Student vets do not always plan ahead," she said. "They just want to get through their exams. While the solution I found seems obvious to people looking from the outside, I had given very little time to looking ahead." Fiona went on to combine her love for animals and flair for business. Within 3 years she had invested money in a clinic, become a partner and built a thriving practice.

Choosing to Follow My Dream

Fiona Strange

Ever since I can remember I have loved being with animals. And then I was enchanted by the TV series All Creatures Great And Small. So I set my 8 year-old heart on being a vet. Today I am a partner in a vet's practice, but there have been many twists and turns along the way. Several questions also needed answering. First, what courses must I study at school? Would I get the right grades, especially in those subjects that I did not like? Second, if I was going to be a vet, could I also earn a good living? Many answers were uncertain, but I had set my heart on working with animals, so I set out on the journey.

Travelling the road proved challenging. Yes, I loved working with animals and seemed to be on my way. The veterinary studies went okay but, before completing my exams I faced a dilemma. Becoming a vet had been my dream and now it was so close. But could I really earn a living doing what I loved?

My husband worked at Microsoft and I took a temporary job at the company. During this time I had the opportunity to organise some career coaching sessions they were holding for all their staff – so I tried some of the tools! The My Future Options exercises asked me to draw all my possibilities. Looking at the map I had drawn in front of me – complete with pluses and minuses – the way ahead seemed obvious. Yes, I loved working with animals. At the same time, however, I really liked the idea of running a business. Of course it was possible to combine the two – if I ran my own practice.

Yes, I know that from the outside this seems logical. But when you are a vet student, it is such a relief to get through the course that students don't often consider their careers. I mean, you'll be a vet, isn't that enough? So I threw myself back into the work. Lots of blood, sweat, late-night revising and splatterings of manure later, I was deemed fit to be sworn into the Royal College of Veterinary Surgeons. I started my first job as a small animal practitioner, managing to keep my head above water for the first year. It's all a new graduate can hope for!

Several events happened that then helped me enormously. I adopted a stray spaniel pup – called Sprocket – who reminded me every day what it's like to dearly love a pet. This helped me to relate better to my worried clients. My boss, Tim, gave me a shot at running one of his branch practices and my husband, Darren, gave me tremendous emotional support. Eighteen months later, my branch practice was thriving. Why? It's sometimes a shock for the public to realise that vets must be business-minded as well as caring for their pets. Can the two go together?

My philosophy is to promote the best healthcare for the pet – because that can also increase the loving bond between the pet and the owner. Imagine a simple consultation to clip a dog's nails. If I also do a quick health check – involving looking at the weight chart – we might consider the dog's diet. We have a dog 'weight-watcher scheme' at the clinic, so the owner may want to enrol their pet in that class. If they then proceed with weight-watchers, their dog will lose weight, become a happier, healthier creature, live longer and give their owner even more pleasure. The clinic will also have benefited because the owner bought the dog's diet food from us and returned for regular weigh-ins.

Last year I was given the chance to buy half of the practice – thus making me a partner. Then came the opportunity to open a second practice in another part of the county – building it from scratch. One year later our team is growing and we have added an extra nurse and practice manager. On the money front, we have managed to break even – that is good in the first year. Planning permission has been give for an extension that will increase the practice space by nearly 50%. I hope to keep on expanding the business until we have a few more thriving clinics and increased the number of healthy, happy pets in Berkshire. We are building a customer focused and healthy business.

Sprocket keeps reminding me of my real motivation for becoming a vet – helping both the pet and the owner. Sometimes you simply have to go back to your ethics. Some older people have very limited money, for example, yet will do almost anything for their pet. That is when you have to find a real 'win-win'. It's been a long journey from watching All Creatures Great And Small, but it has also been extremely enjoyable.

How can you pursue the fulfilling road and get funding? Bearing in mind your strengths, here are some guidelines you may wish to consider:

You can clarify what you can deliver to sponsors.

Imagine you are offering your services to leaders in an organisation. What can you deliver to potential employers? Decision makers are continually trying to improve the 3 P's: their profits, product quality – or service quality – and people. How can you help them to improve one or more of the 3 P's? You may want to tackle the later exercise called *The MD Question.* If you were the Managing Director, what would you hire yourself to deliver? When formulating your offering, it is vital to see the world from the potential sponsors' point of view. Looking at the world from their perspective, ask yourself:

- What are the key challenges facing their organisations? What are the burning issues that keep them awake at night? What must their organisations do to stay ahead of the field?

- What are the specific results they want delivered? What is their picture of success?

- How can what I offer help them to succeed?

If you wish, try tackling the later exercise called *Satisfying Potential Future Sponsors.* This invites you to clarify the challenges facing sponsors and how you can help them to succeed. People buy benefits. Whether you aim to work within your present company or explore the wider market, be crystal clear on what you can offer to a business. Then summarise this by saying:

"The three key things I can deliver for a sponsor are:

1) ....

2) ....

3) ...."

You can clarify your perfect customer

Soon we will explore how to reach potential sponsors. Before then, however, let's step back for a moment. While it may seem unrealistic to be choosy – especially if you don't yet have any customers – it is useful to clarify your perfect target group. During your career you will find customers with whom: a) there is a personal and professional 'click'; b) there is a professional click; c) there is no click at all. We work best with kindred spirits – people who share similar professional values. We can then start off at 7/10 – which provides a springboard for getting to 10/10. If you wish, try tackling the later exercise called *My Perfect Customer*. Ask yourself:

- Who are the people with whom I work best? Who are my favourite customers? Which customers give me positive energy? What are the values of these customers? What are their personality characteristics?

- Do I work best with people in certain fields, for example, high tech, retail, leisure or finance? Do I prefer working in rising businesses – where people are making the new rules – or established businesses? Do I work best with people in certain roles, for example, decision makers, managers, knowledge workers, managers, front-liners or other people?

"But what about other customers," somebody may ask. "We can't always pick and choose. How do you provide them with great service?"

The basic rules apply when working with your favourite or most difficult customers. Be super professional and 'tune into' their agenda. Before any meeting it is vital: a) To prepare properly; b) To put yourself in their shoes, understand their aspirations and understand their picture of success; c) To contact them ahead of time and make clear contracts about the agenda; d) To rehearse all the possible scenarios; e) To spend lots of time revisiting your repertoire and thinking about how you can help them to be successful; f) To, when you actually meet, double-check their agenda for the session; g) To then do everything possible to help them to reach their goals. The key to building a long-term business, however, is to identify and work with your perfect customers.

You can, if appropriate, clarify the type of manager with whom you work best

"But what if you are a full-time employee working in an organisation – do similar rules apply?" somebody may ask. Yes, but it is crucial to find a good manager. After all, they are your key sponsor. So be crystal clear on the type of manager with whom you work best. Different leaders have different leadership styles – and each style has consequences.

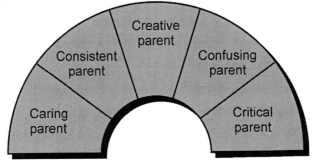

Leaders can choose to behave, for example, as:

a)   Caring Parent. They create an encouraging environment and people like working for them.

b)   Consistent Parent. They give clear messages and people know where they stand. Such leaders can also be challenging, but in a fair way.

c)   Creative Parent. They can be exciting, but also unpredictable.

d)   Confusing Parent. They give double messages or confused messages. People don't know where they stand.

e)   Critical Parent. They continually criticise people, who may find it difficult to work for them.

People often do their best work with managers who are caring and consistent. Many leave organisations because they can't get on with their boss. So find somebody you respect who allows you to do great work. Try tackling the later exercise on this theme called *My Good Manager.*

You can clarify how to reach potential sponsors

How can you find sponsors? If you are out of work and search for a full-time role in an organisation, for example, there is both good news and bad news. The bad news is that old-style methods of job search resemble a lottery and can destroy your self-confidence. Don't rely on applying for jobs that are advertised, because around 250 other candidates are vying for that position. CV's seldom show your full abilities and may not get past the gatekeeper. Recruitment agencies can be okay, but don't expect personal attention. Pressurised to hit targets, they may be tempted to find you a job where they quickly bag their commission. Retain old-style methods as part of your repertoire, but see anything you get as a bonus.

The good news is that 'people buy people'. "More than 90% of my work comes from my network," said one freelancer. "The hard part is getting started. You must spend masses of time visiting people, sharing know-how and helping them to succeed. Providing you keep planting seeds, sooner or later somebody will say: 'How can we take this further?' You make clear contracts, do superb work and deliver success. Then you just keep networking."

How to begin your search? Start by drawing a map of your network. (See the later exercise called *My Network*.) "But I don't know many people," is a common response. If you are employed, write the names of key people in your present organisation. Who have you worked with in the past? Who would hire you again? Who do you admire? Who has left the organisation to move onto fresh fields? Who have become decision makers? Who have you had contact with in the past 10 years? Who might they know? Continue drawing until you have at least 20 names in your network.

Now comes the creative part. How to find a way to contact potential sponsors? Some people suggest cold calling or direct mail, but I believe it is important to be a giver, rather than a taker. Three rules are worth bearing in mind when building and maintaining your network. It is vital:

a)   To reach out to people in a way that fits your values system.

b)   To recognise that real networking is about helping other people to succeed – it is not about self-promotion.

c)   To meet people face-to-face, explore the challenges they face and share knowledge that will help them to succeed.

How to make this happen? Do something every day to keep in touch with people in your network. Do it as early as possible during the day – because this creates positive momentum. Plant lots of seeds, but be patient. It may take up to a year of investing time in potential sponsors before the right opportunity appears. Recognise that people buy face-to-face, so find a way to visit people. Remember that most of your future work will come from present customers. So if you have a 2 pm appointment with a current customer, for example, arrive at 12.00. Sit in their Atrium or restaurant and do your e-mails. Individuals you have met before will come up and say: "I was thinking about you the other day, can you help us with......"

Do things that put a spring in your step. Network in a way that feels right for you. As a writer, for example, it's natural for me to send people free copies of the latest exercise, article or book. Find your way. You may want to recommend books, gift a session on a customer's away day, put people in your network in touch with each other or whatever. Try tackling the later exercise on this theme called *My Natural Way Of Networking.* The key rule remains:

When meeting potential sponsors, it is always about them, it is never about you.

So you may ask them: "What are the key challenges you face? What is your picture of success?" Do some creative problem solving and share ideas that will help them to succeed. Great account directors focus on Credibility, Connection and Concrete Results. They establish credibility with the customer, connect with the customer's aspirations and help them to achieve concrete results. Providing you plant enough seeds, eventually somebody will say: "How can we take this further?" which brings us to the next step.

You can make clear contracts with sponsors – then produce some quick successes

Contracting is crucial. You can clarify: a) The 'What': the specific results they want delivered. b) The 'How': the way that, within parameters, they would like the results delivered. Clarify the Dos and Don'ts for working well with them. Agree on the 3 A's: Accountability, Autonomy and Authority. You are prepared to be accountable, but you also need the appropriate autonomy and authority to deliver the goods. c) The 'When': the deadline for producing the goods.

Conclude the contracting session by 'playing back' what you believe to be the 'What', 'How' and 'When'. Make sure you are both agreed on the picture of success. Say how you will proactively keep them informed and follow-up the meeting by re-confirming the contract in writing. Remember you are still on trial, so produce some quick successes. Getting some early wins will reassure your sponsor and also buy you time.

"But what about money?" somebody may say. "I feel uncomfortable asking for payment." Be prepared to invest a lot of free time up-front. When you feel it is appropriate, however, raise the issue of payment. Some superb sales people never mention 'money'. They use phrases like: "Is it possible to get any funding?" This approach can be surprisingly successful.

Duncan Reid followed these rules when moving from an organisation to becoming a freelancer. He describes this transition in his piece called *My Journey From Corporate Life To Self-Employment*. Duncan gives an honest account of the ups-and-downs involved – because it was not all sweetness and light. Most new work came from his network – but it did not happen straight away. People who leave organisations after being made redundant, for example, find that it is vital 'to make getting a job a full-time time job'. Things don't just happen – you have to make them happen. Assuming you have set your specific goals and found sponsors, let's move onto the next step.

My Journey From Corporate Life to Self-Employment

Duncan Reid

February 1st, 2002. That was the day I took my first steps on an exhilarating journey into the unknown. My corporate career had spanned almost 20 years, the last 10 being for a large software company. Despite still having great respect for the business, I realised I was becoming rather stale. The tell-tale signs were beginning to show. I just didn't get the same buzz. My energy and creativity were low. So I needed to do something before I became a liability to my employer and myself.

I had decided to leave some six months earlier. So why did it take half a year to move-on from the company? Finishing is one of the key skills in life – so it was important to make an elegant exit. Being in the middle of a project, I needed to finish if properly – both for the company and myself. Cutting and running is not for me. (After all, I might want them as a future client!)

On reflection, it is fascinating that I delivered my best work ever during those last six months. Perhaps in the knowledge I was leaving, I felt liberated. And, with that weight lifted, I could do great work. Unconcerned about my next review grade, I could speak up, putting across my views positively and honestly. (I had always had a reputation for being outspoken, but it is amazing how enjoyable it is to have no other agenda than to make the project succeed.) My part of the project completed, I left the comforting arms of corporate life.

"What is your plan?" people asked. Conventional wisdom says that you should at least have: a) A plan or a set of goals; b) Three clients already lined up. So I broke the rules. My 'plan' was to sail rudderless for a little while. Savings could see me through for several months. So I took time-out to do all the things that always need doing but never get done, like gardening and decorating. I even did some travelling. Most people explore exotic warm places, like Australia or South-East Asia. I spent four winter days in Sweden, consulting on a project that equipped troubled teenagers to build aeroplanes!

Three months of paintbrushes and garden forks were enough. Certainly I found activities to fill the day but, after a point, I was killing time, practising that well honed art of constructive avoidance. And I was bored – missing the intellectual challenge and stimulation of working with great people. Savings can only go so far, and mine were coming to an end. I needed a regular income to pay the mortgage.

Reflecting back on those 3 months, they were incredibly important. Some people call it 're-centring' or 're-shaping'. For me it was 'purging'. If I was going to do my own thing, I wanted to clear my mind. A new modus operandi was required, which meant unlearning the old way of operating. Sitting at home, I could no longer dial another corporate extension to get stuff done. Sales, marketing, research & development – they now all lay within my own remit.

Exploring the future, I confronted the questions faced by all budding freelancers. What am I going to do? What is my product or service? What can I offer that people and companies will pay for? How can I help them to be successful? These are hard questions. Frustrated, I looked inward, trying to understand what I did best. Certainly I had some ideas, but these needed translating in a concise and compelling message. Buyers would pay for 'deliverables', not some vague offering. Looking for clues, I focused on my strengths.

My previous company placed a huge emphasis on mentoring and coaching. Why? They wanted people to take charge of their own development – but recognised the value in providing assistance in finding creative solutions to challenges. Selected as one of the mentors, I thoroughly enjoyed the work and got positive feedback. In Gallup's Strengthfinder, 'relator' is my top strength. I love building relationships with people, passing-on knowledge and helping them to be successful. In my time off, I also did voluntary youth work which gave a great sense of fulfilment. So that was it. I was going to be a mentor – offering mentoring and coaching services to companies. Suddenly, however, the world was full of mentors, coaches and consultants. Would anyone employ me? Then one key point hit me: I was a practitioner with many years of hands-on experience in tough businesses. How could I capitalise on this asset?

This was a wobbly time – a very wobbly time. Setting-out on a journey, sometimes you lose your compass and want to return 'home'. Tempted to return to the safety of the corporate fold, I very nearly succumbed. But around me I had some encouraging and supportive people. Taking time-out to talk with them was vital. Setting-off into the 'jungle', I considered myself as an intrepid explorer on a journey of discovery, beating a track through the wilderness. Perhaps I was, but only in my head. Luckily, guardian angels were around me. They did not show me the path, because it must be my path, but picked me up and dusted me down when necessary. So I plodded on…And then the work came. Mainly, of course, from people I knew in my network.

Certainly I knew the theory: 'Most of your work will come from people who know you'. Now I found it to be true. Emerging from my sanctuary, I reached-out to people I knew. Results took time, but then I struck gold. A previous colleague from the software firm was now implementing a pilot project for a High Street company. They needed somebody to maintain the service levels in the old centre, whilst also transferring operations to the new site. Many people in the old site were facing uncertainty. So could we maintain the morale and service standards? Luckily, my background as a practitioner helped, and I acted as the interim manager for several months. The business results were paramount: but the mentoring experience helped when encouraging people to shape their futures.

"But you were a project manager," somebody may say. "What about being a mentor. Shouldn't you have waited until the right opportunity appeared?" Like an actor, I needed to work – not only for my soul, but also to pay the mortgage. The interim management role took 3 or 4 days a week and, within it, I was able to practice coaching and mentoring. Lucrative projects do not come knocking on the door – so I had to get out and meet other potential customers. The network paid off again.

After several months, I had expanded the portfolio career. By then I was: a) Doing the interim management; b) Coaching employees on the company's new site; c) Working on the customer service offering with a high tech company; d) Building a working relationship with a communications company. (The latter became the main source of my income several months later.) Nowadays I spend most of my time doing one-to-one coaching and mentoring.

Looking back, I probably did not realise the emotions I would experience on the journey from corporate life to self-employment. People tell you that it will be a switch-back ride – but some switch-backs are exhilarating and others are frightening. (Whichever one you take, at least you feel alive!) So what have been the take-away lessons? Here are the notes that I would like to have written to myself at the start of the journey.

1) Take responsibility for everything

Working for a corporation, you are part of a big team. You can call on the experts in marketing, finance or IT. As a freelancer, at least in the beginning, you must do all these activities yourself, which can be both daunting and enlightening. For example, I needed a way to bill companies for my services i.e. get paid. But there were many choices: sole trader, limited company, partnership, limited liability partnership. In the end, I went for a limited company. Many businesses like to deal with partners who are limited companies and there was something reassuring about having my liability limited.

2) Clarify what you can offer to customers – and how it can help them to be successful

Providing mentoring and coaching was seductive, but I was up against a lot of competition. Looking at my corporate track record, there was a pattern of running projects successfully. Initially I found this to be the best way into companies who wanted to improve their results. After establishing credibility, it was possible to then offer them coaching. Companies bought it because they wanted their staff to be self-managing, make good decisions and develop a sustainable business.

3) Spend a lot of time reaching out to customers

This part of the journey can be long and disheartening. Legwork is crucial. Virtually everybody buys 'face-to-face', which means lots of travel. Like many people, I underestimated the time it takes to get the work, do the work and get the money in the bank. Setbacks are natural, so just keep going. When you get turned down, don't take it personally. Learn from the experience and get straight back into the driving seat. When meeting potential customers, it might not be a "no", more a "not now". As time went by – plus many meetings with potential customers – more work came in. Some of the "not nows" became "now, please". I was delighted, but quite determined that I wasn't going to get complacent.

4) Develop a support network

Most work came from people I knew already. It was simply a question of contacting them in the appropriate way – focusing on how to help them, rather than promote myself. In addition, however, I gained enormously from having supporters around me. One or two gave me a 'kick' when appropriate – being a Scottish football supporter, I have occasional periods of worrying reflection – whilst others opened doors to potential new clients.

5) Deliver success

Maybe it is because I like excitement, but I approach every piece of work as if it is my last. As a freelancer you have to deliver 100% all the time. If you don't produce what your sponsors want, you don't get paid. You have nowhere to hide. But I love the excitement. The challenge spurs me on and I am always looking for ways to improve.

Finally, develop a name and a brand. Now, I'm not necessarily the most creative person, but I did have an inkling. Mentoring and coaching were my main offerings – so the word 'mentor' ought to figure. Trawling the business literature, there were hundreds of companies in the field. So I decided on something different – hence Paradise Mentors Ltd was born. "That's not a business-like name," some people argued. Maybe, but at least it is an opening discussion point. (I'm not going to reveal where the "Paradise" part comes from, except that it is inspired by one of my biggest passions in life – football.)

Perhaps I have been fortunate, but the company is now expanding. The projects have got bigger – so I have joined forces with somebody I have known for many years. Another practitioner, she has run many successful transformation projects. This period of my career is exciting and invigorating. It's a thrill to go to work every morning, even if that particular journey is just to my desk at home to write a report or call some clients. So will I ever go back to being a corporate man? "Never say never," people say. But the answer to that question is: "Not right now – I'm having too much of a ball."

c) *You can clarify your strategy*

Let's imagine you have settled on your specific goals – the 'What'. The next stage is to clarify the 'How'. Many people have visions, but few turn them into visible results. Successful individuals and teams follow similar principles towards reaching their goals. They know what mountain they are climbing, how they are climbing it and when they will reach the summit. You can follow these principles in your own way. Try tackling the later exercise called *Successful Strategies*. After settling on your specific goals, clarify your key strategies – the 'How' – by asking yourself:

"What are the three key things I can do to give myself the greatest chance of success?"

Why so few strategies? Concentrating on a few principles focuses the mind. Simon Walker, the Toshiba skipper, encouraged the crew to focus on their core values: 'Safe, Happy and Fast.' There may be many 'sub-strategies', of course, but its good to have a few key principles. Beware of big organisations that communicate 57 strategies that nobody can remember. After settling on your 'What' and the 'How', it's time to integrate these into your project plan – the 'When'.

How to create your action plan? Peak performers frequently start from their destination and work backwards. So try tackling the later exercise called *My Picture of Perfection: The road map towards achieving the goals.* Pick a date in the future and describe the specific results you want to achieve by that date. For example: "I will have created that book, delivered that project, launched that product or whatever." Working backwards, describe the specific things you want to deliver at each milestone along the journey. If appropriate, also write the *actual words* you want to hear people saying. Keep going until you arrive back at the present day. You now have the road map towards achieving your picture of perfection.

Pause for a moment. Double check your project plan. What can you do today? What can you do tomorrow? How can you get some early wins? Let's move onto the next stage – working hard to achieve your picture of success.

(The strengths approach can also be applied to building super teams. During the past 40 years I have had the opportunity to work with many great teams. Some of the lessons from working with these are summarised in the piece called *The Art of Building Super Teams*.)

The Art of Building Super Teams

People can combine their talents to build great teams Super teams are special. They start by having a compelling purpose and translate this into a clear picture of perfection. People know what mountain they are climbing; why they are climbing it and when they will reach the summit. Super teams are made-up of volunteers – not victims. People proactively opt-in and make their best contribution towards achieving the goals. They do professional work, solve problems and deliver peak performance. Super teams do everything possible to achieve their picture of perfection.

So how can you build such a team? Imagine you are taking-over a team or a company. There are many ways to climb a mountain. Similarly, there are many ways to build a team. The super teams approach comes with two health warnings. First, it works. On paper it looks simple, but that does not mean it is easy. Second, it calls for taking tough decisions, especially about people. They must be positive, proactive and professional.

How can you decide about the people you want in the team? Keep asking yourself The Freelance Question. "If everybody in the team left today and offered their services back as freelancers: a) Who would I hire? b) What would I hire them to deliver? Bearing these answers in mind, what must I do to build a super team?" Ask yourself this every day, and act on the answers. If you are serious about achieving results, there is zero-tolerance for negativity. Remember, however, that you want people who are characters, not clones. Let's explore the steps you can take towards building a super team.

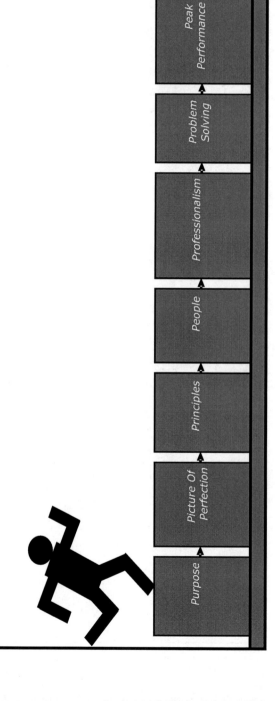

SUPER TEAMS

People choose to be in the team. They then focus on the following steps towards achieving peak performance.

Purpose → Picture Of Perfection → Principles → People → Professionalism → Problem Solving → Peak Performance

Step 1: Purpose

Great teams have a crystal-clear purpose. They commit themselves to achieving a compelling cause that gets people out of bed in the morning. They may aim, for example; to find a cure for AIDS: to win the Ryder Cup; to invent an exciting product; to deliver 100% customer satisfaction or whatever. What is your team's purpose? Try writing it on a Post-It Note. "The purpose of our team is:......" Dare to be honest. If the aim is simply to make lots of money, tell people. Don't wrap it in nice-sounding intentions. Practice what you preach. If you are honest about the purpose, people will decide if they want to sign-up to the cause.

Step 2: Picture of Perfection

Great leaders translate the purpose into a crystal clear picture of perfection. They also draw a road map towards achieving the goal. (See illustration). Start from your destination and work backward. Pick a date in the future. Describe the actual things that will be happening then that show the team has reached its goals. Draw a road map of the milestones along the way, describing the specific things that will be happening on the journey. If you wish, describe the 'actual words' you will be hearing. For example: What will your key sponsors, customers and team members be saying? Show the benefits of reaching the goal – because people buy benefits – then move onto the next step.

THE PICTURE OF PERFECTION

The Goal Is:

To.....................................

The date is:	The specific things we will have achieved by then will be:	The words we want to hear people saying then are:
*...............................	*..	".."
*............................	*..	".."
*............................	*..	".."
*............................	*..	".."
*............................	*..	".."

Step 3:   Principles

Great teams focus on the key principles – strategies – that will give them the greatest chance of success. People need to know the game plan, so keep it to a few main strategies. Beware of companies that cascade 57 point plans. They have often forgotten their purpose and, instead, replaced it with a process. The centre actually starts believing the process is the purpose and fills everybody's diaries with internal meetings. Communicate the purpose, the picture of perfection and the key principles. Everybody will then know 'What' the team is aiming to achieve; 'Why' they are aiming to achieve it; and 'How' they aim to reach the goals. Then move onto the next step.

Step 4:   People

This is the pivotal part. Great leaders will communicate the purpose, picture of perfection and principles – but without the right people they are sunk. Get the right people with the right spirit. Great teams are built on 'Similarity of Spirit and Diversity of Strengths'. (Diversity of spirit is a recipe for disaster.) Get the right balance between 'Soul Players' and 'Star Players'. Soul Players embody the spirit of the team. They are consistent players who do the right things day after day. Star Players also embody the spirit, but add that 'little bit extra'. (There is no place for 'Semi-Detached' Players who are waiting to be understood or motivated.) You need people who are positive, proactive and professional. One negative person can dilute the energy of 100 people in a team.

Clear contracting is crucial and is the hallmark of great cultures. First: Communicate the picture of perfection. Second: Invite people to proactively get back to you and show how they want to contribute towards achieving the picture of perfection. Third: Bearing in mind each person's strengths, make clear contracts with them on their part in reaching the goals. Once this is finalised, gather the whole team together and repeat the process. After giving the big picture, invite each person – or, in a large group, each team – to share their part in achieving the goal. Then move onto the next step.

Step 5:   Professionalism

Great teams have good habits. Following the daily disciplines, they always achieve at least a 7/10. "Maybe I just need reassuring," you may say, "but how can I ensure that people achieve the required professional standards?" First: Hire people who are responsible, self-managing and deliver on their promises. Second: Invite each person – or, in larger groups, each team – to describe the specific things they will do to always deliver the 7/10. Third: Ask them to proactively keep you informed about the actions they are taking to tackle issues that are in the Green, Amber and Red Zones. Providing people deliver results, then leave them alone. Your role is to shape tomorrow's business; the self-managing people will take care of today's business. You will need all your energy to tackle the next step.

Step 6:   Problem Solving

Great teams contain many resilient people who have the ability to overcome setbacks. They are also good decision-makers – especially under pressure. Faced by a challenge, they begin by staying calm and clarifying the real results to achieve. They then explore the possible choices, consequences and creative solutions. Committing *to their chosen solution, they work hard to achieve concrete results. Good leaders also recognise that: "Results require proper rest and recovery." So they encourage people to take time-out to relax, re-centre and refocus. They need time to recharge their batteries, but also focus on 'course correction'. Taking the helicopter view, they can ensure they are on-track for achieving the picture of perfection. People who apply the wisdom learned from both successes and setbacks are more likely to take the next step.*

Step 7: Peak Performance

Great teams finish. They deliver the goods when it matters. People keep working hard, overcome setbacks and achieve the picture of perfection. Sometimes they reach their goals by adding that 'touch of class'. They move from 7/10 to 10/10 and become 'A Class Act'. "Great teams," we are told, "produce great performances on great occasions."

One ending is a new beginning. Some teams disband after reaching the goal. Other teams refocus on the purpose, then translate it into a new picture of perfection. Pacesetting teams, for example, have a special kind of psychology. They aim to take the lead, maintain the lead and extend the lead. Staying ahead of everybody else, they make the new rules for the game. Guiding your team to success, you may then want to repeat the process. As they say in sport: "First build a team, then a club, then a dynasty." That calls for making even tougher decisions, of course, on the road towards building a second-generation Super Team.

Specific Goals:

Trigger Questions

The following pages provide trigger questions that a person can consider to clarify their specific goals, sponsors and strategy.

a) Specific Goals

- Everybody is different and has different views of success. What is your picture of success? Imagine you are 80 and looking back on your life. Describe 3 things you will have done that for you will mean your life has been successful. What do you want to be your legacy? What do you want to pass on to people?

- Let's take a reality check before finalising your goals. Some things you can control and some you can't. So let's focus on how you can 'control the controllables'. Looking at your life and work: a) What are the things you can control? b) What are the things you can't control? c) How can you build on what you can control and manage what you can't?

- Looking to the future, what are the possible roads you can travel?

  Try tackling the exercise 'My Possible Options'. Make a map of the possible routes you can take in the next couple of years. Describe the pluses and minuses of each option. Rate the attractiveness of each option. Do this on a scale 0 – 10. Be creative and consider other routes. For example, is it possible to combine the best parts of each road into a new option? Settle on the route you want to travel.

  Finally, ask yourself: "Will pursuing this route – and reaching the specific goal – contribute towards achieving my long-term picture of success?"

- If you are interested in finding potential sponsors – people who will hire you for doing what you do best – you may want to explore the next stage. If not, go straight to the section on 'Strategy'.

b) *Sponsors*

- Let's explore how you might find potential sponsors. The key will be to offer a service or product that will help them to succeed.

  Looking at the world from the sponsor's point of view, what are the key challenges they face? What is their picture of perfection? Decision makers are often concerned about improving the 3 Ps. They continually want to improve their profits, their product quality – service quality – and their people. How can what you offer help sponsors to improve one or more of the 3 Ps?

- Let's consider how you might find potential sponsors. People buy people. So we can begin by drawing your network. Who do you know in your present organisation who might be interested in what you offer? Who do you know who has left the organisation? Who do you know from your past? Write the names of any other people who might know somebody who could be interested in what you offer.

- How can you reach your network in a way that fits your values system – in a way that feels comfortable? Real networking is about helping other people to succeed, it is not about self-promotion. Bearing this in mind, how can you help people in your network? How can pass on know-how, tools or other things which they can use to reach their goals?

- Providing you reach out to enough people, eventually somebody will say: 'How can we take this further?' Clear contracting will then be crucial. Agree with them on 'What' is to be delivered, 'How' and by 'When'. Make sure you have the right balance of accountability, autonomy and authority. How can you 'play back' your understanding so that both you and the sponsors are agreed on the same picture? Finally, you will still be on 'trial', so how can you get some quick successes to reassure the sponsor?

c) *Strategy*

- Let's explore the strategy for reaching your goals. The vision is the 'What'; the strategy is the 'How'. Bearing in mind the goals you want to achieve, what are the three key things you can do to give yourself the greatest chance of success? Decide on your top three strategies. Then, taking each one in turn, describe the specific things you can do to implement that strategy.

- Let's pull everything together into your project plan. If you wish, try tackling the exercise called 'My Picture of Perfection: The road map towards achieving the goals'. Start from your destination and work backwards. Pick a date in the future and describe the results you want to achieve by that date. If appropriate, describe the actual words you want to hear people saying. Working backwards, describe what you want to deliver at each stage of the journey. Keep going until you reach the present day.

- Before setting off on the journey, take a moment to consider the potential consequences. What will be the pluses of achieving the goals – both for you and for other people? What will be the possible minuses? How can you maximise the pluses and minimise the minuses? Are you prepared to accept the whole package? On a scale 0 – 10, how committed do you feel to reaching the goal? What can you do today? What can you do tomorrow? How can you get some early wins?

Specific Goals

Exercises

The following pages provide exercises that
a person can use to clarify their specific goals.

Success

Looking back when I am 80, I will feel my life has been successful if I have done the following things:

- ....

....

....

- ....

....

....

- ....

....

....

- ....

....

....

My White Room

Imagine your life is an empty White Room with nothing in it except your family. Starting afresh, you can put what you want in your White Room. List the 3 people, 3 strengths, 3 goals, 3 possessions and 3 other things you would put in your White Room. Then take steps to concentrate on these energy-givers in your present life.

The 3 People

- ....

- ....

- ....

The 3 Strengths

- ....

- ....

- ....

The 3 Goals

- ....

- ....

- ....

The 3 Possessions

- ....
- ....
- ....

The 3 Other Things

- ....
- ....
- ....

My Controllables

Can Control.
The things I can control are:

- ....

- ....

- ....

Can't Control.
The things I can't control are:

- ....

- ....

- ....

Controlling the Controllables.
The things I can do to build on what I can control
– and manage what I can't control – are to:

- ....

- ....

- ....

My Network

Draw a map of your personal network. Start with the people you know best, plus any customers, then expand your map. List everybody who might buy your products or put you in touch with potential customers.

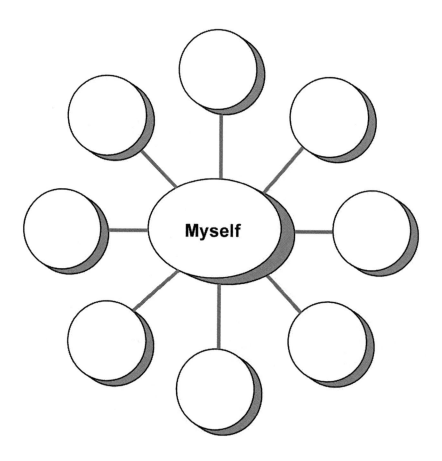

My Natural Way of Networking

**The ways of keeping in touch with my
network that come naturally for me are to:**

- ....

- ....

- ....

**The steps I can take to keep in touch with
my network by following these ways are to:**

- ....

- ....

- ....

The MD Question

If I was a Managing Director, the specific things I would hire myself to deliver would be to:

1) ....

....

....

2) ....

....

....

3) ....

....

....

Satisfying My Present Sponsors

The sponsor's name is:

- ....

Looking at the world from their point of view, the specific results they want delivered are:

- ....

- ....

- ....

The Dos & Don'ts for working with this sponsor are:

Do:

- ....

- ....

- ....

- ....

Don't:

- ....
- ....
- ....

Satisfying The Sponsor.
Bearing in mind these answers, the things
I can do to satisfy this sponsor are to:

- ....
- ....
- ....

Satisfying Potential Future Sponsors

The sponsor's name is:

- ....

The specific results they want delivered are:

- ....

- ....

- ....

The challenges they face are:

- ....

- ....

- ....

The Dos & Don'ts for working with this sponsor are:

Do:

- ....

- ....

- ....

- ....

Don't:

- ....

- ....

- ....

Satisfying The Sponsor.
Bearing in mind these answers, the things I can do to satisfy this sponsor are to:

- ....

- ....

- ....

My Perfect Customer

The characteristics of my perfect customer are:

- ....
- ....

The role and industry of my perfect customer are:

- ....
- ....

The aspirations of my perfect customer are:

- ....
- ....

The specific things I can offer to help my perfect customer to achieve their picture of success are:

- ....
- ....

My Good Manager

My Previous Good Managers

The good managers I have had in the past – and the qualities in each of these – have been:

1) ....

The things that made them a good manager were:

- They..

- They..

- They..

2) ....

The things that made them a good manager were:

- They..

- They..

- They..

<u>My Good Manager</u>

The qualities I want in a manager are for them:

- ....

- ....

- ....

My Action Plan

The steps I can take to increase the chances of finding
such a manager – or managers – in the future are to:

- ....

- ....

- ....

My Possible Options

Start by drawing the possible routes you can take in the future. Follow this by listing the pluses and minuses of each route – together with the attractiveness of each option. Then move onto the next stage – your preferred option.

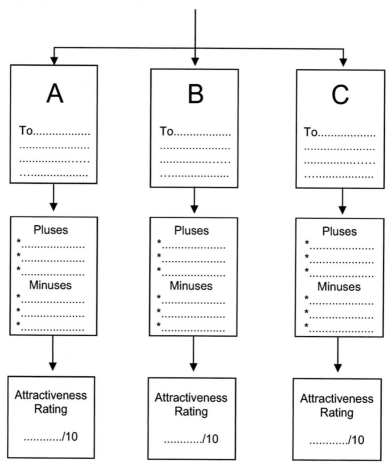

My Preferred Option

**The route – or combination of
routes – I would like to pursue is to:**

● ....

**The pluses of pursuing this route –
both for myself and other people – are:**

● ....

The possible minuses are:

● ....

The steps I can take to pursue this route are to:

● ....

● ....

● ....

Successful Strategies

Bearing in mind the specific goals I want to achieve, the three key things I can do to give myself the greatest chance of success are to:

1) ....

....

2) ....

....

3) ....

....

My Picture of Perfection: The road map towards achieving the goals

The specific goals I want
to achieve by .... are to:

- ....

The date is:	The specific things that will have been achieved by then will be:	The *actual words* I want to hear people saying are:
•	•	" .... "
	•	
•	•	" .... "
	•	
•	•	" .... "
	•	

STEP 3:

SUCCESS

Everybody can work hard to achieve their picture of success. "I love to 'sweat'," said one person. "I love to become totally absorbed in the activity. Sometimes I love the journey as much as reaching the goal. Time goes away and I feel, 'This is what I was meant to do.' So how do you get started? 'Get an early success,' is the advice – then develop good habits. Peak performers overcome setbacks on the journey and work hard to reach their goals. Providing they fulfil their purpose, they may experience a sense of peace.

The Strengths Way is about encouragement and using your strengths to help others to succeed. Tamara and Jonas Himmelstrand pursued this route when embarking on pioneering treatment for their son, Jakob. Both feel passionately about nurturing people's talents – and they express this life-theme in many different ways. Tamara works as an innovative violin teacher. Born and raised in Switzerland, she trained as a violinist at the Conservatoire in Lausanne. The concept of the 'inner violin' captured her imagination and she developed a joyful method for enabling students to play in an authentic way. Jonas has worked as an educator, mentor and writer for the past 25 years. Another way they express their passion is described in their story *Our Journey With Our Son Jakob*. They set the scene by writing:

"Like all parents, we want to give our children the best possible start in life. Jakob, our first child, was born in 1994. He seemed to grow up normally, except for a deeply introverted expression. Slow in learning to talk, he was extremely sensitive to chaotic surroundings. As good parents, we listened, supported and tried to help our son. As time passed by, however, it was clear something was not right. Finally, at the age of 5, Jakob was diagnosed as having infantile autism, which is a severe mental handicap in communicating to others."

Our Journey With Our Son Jakob
Tamara & Jonas Himmelstrand

Every parent wants the best for their children. Every child is special – so every journey with every child is special. Like all parents, we want to give our children the best possible start in life. Jakob, our first child, was born in 1994. He seemed to grow up normally, except for a deeply introverted expression. Slow in learning to talk, he was extremely sensitive to chaotic surroundings. As good parents, we listened, supported and tried to help our son. As time passed by, however, it was clear something was not right. Finally, at the age of 5, Jakob was diagnosed as having infantile autism, which is a severe mental handicap in communicating to others.

This is where our journey began. After being convinced that Jakob's difficulties were a form of autism, our family doctor referred us to specialists at the neuro-psychiatric clinic in Uppsala, Sweden. But the earliest appointment we could get was in 18 months! Time was of the essence, because we knew that it was vital to provide specialist help or training at an early age.

The first step was to pool our strengths. We both have extensive experience in training, teaching and personal development. Jonas is a consultant who encourages people to develop their talents and also passes-on skills they can use to become fine educators. Tamara is a violin teacher who has her own creative teaching method. Both self-starters, we put enormous energy into what we believe-in. Scanning the world for possibilities, we recalled reading about an autistic boy who was completely cured. The BBC had produced a documentary about the method – the Son-Rise programme, based in America. So we went searching on the Internet.

Son-Rise is a perfect values-match to our own training experience. The approach focuses on respect, love and a positive and enthusiastic attitude – plus a very specific way of relating to the autistic child. Son-Rise uses whatever motivation and strengths the autistic child has to start to build communication. (Later we discovered the method offered by our local hospital is an older approach based on behavioural therapy.) The realisation also hit us that, if we took the Son-Rise route, it would require intense daily training 6-10 hours a day, 7 days a week, for years. The decision was made in our hearts, however, and we committed ourselves to the journey with Jakob.

Calling the Son-Rise Institute in Massachusetts, we found them very helpful. This led to us ordering the 'start-up package': some books, an introduction to the Son-Rise methods and instructions on how to set-up the special play room. Jonas also enrolled for the next special training programme in two months time. Getting started immediately, we set-up the special playroom – but with all toys out of Jakob's reach. He needed to ask for anything he wanted – but everything was geared to success.

Our demands on his communication would never be higher than Jakob being able to get what he wanted with a little effort. The message to the child is: "The more you communicate, the faster you get what you want. If you don't want to extend your communication, you get it anyway - because this is a friendly world. It just takes a little longer time." We tried out the playroom and, when Jonas returned from the course in America, we would start the work in earnest. This was already an exciting project in which we could build on everybody's strengths.

Jakob has always had tremendous strengths. We began the Son-Rise programme in June 2000, when he was 5 years-old, and focused on his assets. He is happy, intelligent, visual and has great personal integrity. He will put effort into things he is highly motivated to do – and no energy whatsoever into other tasks. He has always been perfectly physically healthy, has great posture and excellent balance. We aimed to build on these assets.

Jakob's challenges were his total lack of communication skills. When asked a question, he would simply echo the question back. Sometimes this could be quite funny. When going too far out into the water on a beach, we called: "Come back, Jakob". He would simply yell back: "Come back, Jakob," then continue his pursuit of the waves. He did not understand the concepts of 'I' or 'You'. Frequently referring to himself in the third person as 'Jakob', almost as if observing himself from outside. His most advanced statements would be: *"Daddy, buy milk in shop for Jakob". Combined with the inability to differentiate between 'you' and 'I', he would say things like: "Mommy helps you to wash you". He used standardised phrases to get his basics in life, often using questions as requests. For example: "Are you hungry?" meant "I am hungry".*

Communication was not easy, partly because of the almost total lack of eye-contact, which is typical of autistic children. There was no talk back and forth. Sometimes there was a request from Jakob, but he did not understand any request or question put to him. Encountering these challenges, therefore, he had never been able to play with other children – nor did he show interest in his two-year-old sister. But Jakob did talk. He could recite by memory books we had read for him – over and over again for hours, not changing one word. Another autistic trait is extreme sensitivity to many impressions. Within a few minutes visiting a noisy shop, for example, he would get totally out of control and quite literally climb the walls. Whenever we had visitors to the house, he would first see who was coming. Not responding to them, he would leave the room to be alone. So let's look at some of the stages on our journey.

The magic of the special playroom

Jonas returned from the Son-Rise course in America in August 2000. Everything was ready to start – and the first whole day in the special playroom was magic. Every interaction immediately became easier and we connected to our son on a whole new level. Leaving the room after 8 hours, Jakob had a tremendous radiance – as if we parents finally understood his needs. Within a few months he was smiling, which he had never really done before. Jakob began to use a pen to draw and write letters, which previously he had absolutely refused to try. Now there were short moments of play with his sister, Rebecka, and he began to answer questions. At Christmas he retold something he thought was funny from a Donald Duck cartoon. Encouraged by this enormous progress, it was clear the approach was succeeding, which gave us the energy to keep working.

Finding volunteers, a public meeting and a radio interview

Every journey brings challenges and ours were only just starting. We did not have the financial means to give-up our jobs and spend the required 6-10 hours a day in the special room, 7 days a week. Rebecka, our daughter, also needed her share of the family time, so we required help. The Son-Rise programme recommended setting-up a public lecture to recruit volunteers. Such people needed to be carefully selected, trained and coached, however, if their efforts were to bear fruit. And every parent is sensitive to who is going to play with their child in a confined space for 2-3 hours. Jonas set-up a lecture in Uppsala, marketing it through our network and an interview on the local radio station. Twenty-five people showed up, more than expected, and afterwards we seemed to have 3-5 interested volunteers. We were overjoyed.

Son-Rise is demanding on the volunteers. The level of energy, enthusiasm and excitement must be high. They must also be highly attentive. For example, they need to pick-up on the cues regarding when to join the child in an activity and when to lead. Understandably, volunteers can find it hard to give unstinting loving attention to somebody who refuses to communicate. After a few months all but one of our original volunteers had quit. So we approached a social worker: Could we get paid assistants to help? No, but we could get 20 hours per month 'baby-sitting', as a relief for us as parents. We needed people willing to train to be Son-Rise assistants, rather than baby-sitters. So we invited the social worker to our house and presented the programme. Success: we received a letter providing funding for 24 hours a month. We needed 45 hours a week, but it was a start, so we gave the salary to our only volunteer, making her a paid assistant.

More challenges and Solutions

Now it was May 2001. Sweden is a country with many advantages, including a high standard of living for most people. Everybody recognises this must be paid for, which produces a high tax society. One area that is highly taxed, for example, is employing other people. Jonas contemplated trying to expand his business to cover the costs of employing assistants – but would need to at least triple his net income to pay for the 45 hours a week! Sweden is not a volunteer culture and the welfare system is expected to provide help in most cases. The Son-Rise method was little known in Sweden, however, and we had to persuade the local municipality of its merits. This would be difficult and did not play to our strengths.

So we threw ourselves back into practising Son-Rise. During the darkest hours we remembered the statement: "If you find no support, then use your own passion. Support will eventually show up, because passion inspires others." That became our mantra. During the following months we and our assistant gave Jakob as many hours of training as possible. September came and we lost our assistant, who returned to her studies. Jakob was out of control, not getting enough time in the room, and we felt desperate. Then a train of events were set in motion.

- *We learned of another Son-Rise family who had managed to convince the local government to get a solid amount of assistant hours. Hope returned.*

- *Calling the social worker, we became more demanding, saying: "It can't be right that we have to do this all on our own in a high tax society. Besides, other people are getting this support." She listened and agreed. But it would be difficult, because the decision must be made at the political level. She would, however, be willing to help.*

- *Months passed. Calling her again, she said she was working on the case, but requested that we do not call again and disturb her. At home, we hired another volunteer, but they found the task/job/methodology too demanding.*

- *We decided to do another passion push. Building on what we loved to do, we devised a schedule that, when both Jonas and Tamara were at home, gave Jakob six hours in the room every day. The schedule was extremely intricate and strenuous, being timed to the minute. But the pluses outweighed the minuses, compared with Jakob running around the house out of control.*

- *The schedule worked. Jakob became more communicative and we maintained this timetable for two months. Then came a breakthrough.*

A few days before Christmas 2001, Jonas was called to speak at a local government meeting. Despite being given only a few hours notice, he gave the speech of a lifetime. Explaining our schedule, he outlined Jakob's progress. The people seemed deeply touched by what they heard. The outcome was that we got paid assistance for 45 hours a week, our best ever Christmas present. So we sought the right people as assistants. Determined not to repeat our earlier mistakes, we told everybody the job was highly demanding. Twenty or so people showed interest and, after meetings and interviews, we settled on four. Son-Rise demands enormous energy, so 2-3 hours a day is the most you can ask from any individual. Several months of intensive work showed that three of them were up for the job. In fact, two of these are still with us today in November 2004.

Since the beginning of January 2002 we have successfully recruited more assistants. First, they must have a solid psyche to manage the job. Second, they must be encouraged and given great support during the initial training. We start with 10 minutes in the playroom and a few simple instructions - then make extensive use of video feedback. Assistants who embrace the method increase the time slot until, after 4-6 weeks, they spend up to two hours in the room. Jonas, with his background in training, is in charge of the assistant's introduction. Tamara, with her one-to-one talent from violin training, then takes over. She meets every assistant to go through the video feedback once a week, which continues throughout their work with us.

Life goes on and running the programme calls for managing the household effectively. Jakob requires a diet free from gluten, casein, fast carbohydrates and additives. He cannot eat 70% of what is offered in the supermarket. Time is crucial – so preparing a meal can take no longer than 30 minutes, which makes the menu very Spartan. So Jonas, the logistics person, manages the shopping once a week through a custom-made list, which saves hours every month. Tamara, accustomed to timetables from being a violin teacher, maintains the schedule for the assistants, video feedback and 'team meetings'. Maintaining her violin education, she schedules all her pupils for the one day a week when Jonas is home. We keep this lifestyle throughout the year, except for three weeks every summer, when we go to the beautiful island of Gotland in the Baltic Sea. The creative chaos calls for everybody knowing the tasks and priorities. Jakob's progress, however, provides the positive energy that keeps it all together.

Achievements along the journey

The media had given us our first glimpse of Son-Rise, so we wanted to share our story with other people. In early 2002 we called our local newspaper and invited them to write about the programme. They produced two articles, one in February 2002, the other in June 2003. The same journalist wrote both articles and was amazed at Jakob's progress between the two visits. Later, in early 2004, he was ready to attend a normal school class for between one and two hours a week. Now:

- *He can sit for 45 minutes among 23 other children and, when appropriate, be still and quiet.*

- *He can raise his hand, answer questions, communicate his needs, express his feelings and his eye-contact has drastically improved.*

- *His imagination is excellent. He can read, write and do maths – plus his English is superb. He has a passionate interest in cars, rides a horse and, demonstrating a fine ear for music, is teaching himself the piano.*

Jakob is, above all, happy. He has retained his energy, joy and proud posture throughout the intense training programme, proving the deep humanistic roots of the Son-Rise method. He still has challenges: His communication can be clumsy and he is very obsessive about his interests.

Children in the school classroom were polite, but still a bit wary. So the teacher invited Jonas to talk to the class. The children listened and asked many questions. They were touched after realising the difficulties Jakob had been through during the last four years. The next time he and Tamara arrived the class was transformed. The teacher and children received Jakob differently, smiling and saying: "Hello."

Now we face another challenge. The local government is embarking on intensive cost cutting, threatening some of the assistant hours. The only way to maintain these is to appeal through the courts. Sticking to our strengths, we have found an attorney with experience of this particular Swedish law – The Law of Special Support – while we continue doing our Son-Rise programme and documenting our successes. Whatever the outcome of the appeal, we will find some form of solution. So what have we learned on the journey?

- *Follow your values. Overcoming obstacles takes a lot of energy, but we were doing something we really believed in, which provided us with great strength.*

- *Look for alternatives. There are always options, somewhere in the world somebody has probably tried some way that works. If not, then try inventing one yourself. Invest time in finding, or creating, as many options as possible.*

- *Get visible results. Showing visible results has been one of the keys in getting continued support for our programme.*

- *Passion is contagious. Passion and success inspires and attracts other interested people.*

- *Behind every public official is a human being with a heart. No human being can resist love, joy and excitement for any length of time.*

So the journey continues. And we are thankful for all the lessons along the way. But then, as we said at the beginning, every parent's journey with every child is special in its own way.

The journey with Jakob involved traveling from Sweden, where they lived, to the United States. It also involved radical changes in lifestyle. Along the way they learned many lessons they could apply across their lives. These included: "Follow your values. Look for alternatives. Get visible results – especially if you want the state to fund your approach! Passion is contagious: it inspires and attracts other interested people."

So how can you work towards achieving your goals? If you wish, you can focus on four themes: a) You can do superb work; b) You can find solutions to challenges; c) You can help other people to succeed; d) You can achieve your picture of success. Let's explore these themes.

a) *You can do superb work*

Sometimes this can be easier if you are a freelancer. Why? You can spend 100% of your time satisfying customers – rather than attending internal meetings. Good organisations, however, also encourage their people to do great work. Air Miles was one company that embraced this approach during its early days. Directors greeted employees to the company's induction programme by giving the following messages.

"Welcome to the company. You are here because you want to take responsibility, give great service and deliver results. We want to help you to live these values every day. Being in the service business, our job is to provide great service and help our customers to succeed. Being a commercial organisation, of course, we also need to make a profit.

"The company's role is to communicate our purpose and principles. The way you practice these principles is, within parameters, up to you in your part of the business. Try to make sure that whatever you do, however, supports the principles and contributes to achieving the overall purpose. You can use your brains to find 'win-win' solutions for both the customer and the company."

Great workers follow a similar approach. They pursue their passion, translate it into a clear purpose and follow certain principles to be super professional each day. Here are some ideas for doing superb work.

Keep working towards achieving the picture of perfection

Keep following the key strategies. Olympics athletes start by clarifying their picture of perfection. Starting from their destination, they make a project plan. Putting the picture on the wall, they develop a daily rhythm. Why? People like to have a sense of meaning – so it is good to connect today's grunt work with tomorrow's great work. Returning to your picture of success, you may want to do something similar. Keep pursuing the key strategies, develop good habits and get into a rhythm. Get a success early each day – because this creates positive momentum.

Make good use of your prime times – the times of the day when you have most energy. "My best times are between 8.30 and 12.30," said one writer, "then I come alive again after 8.00 at night. Nowadays I protect my prime times – because it is when I am most productive. Previously I tried to push water uphill. Going against my natural rhythm, I criticised myself if I could not write in the afternoon. Nowadays I make good use of the mornings, fix the 'grunt work' in the afternoon – then write again in the evening."

Keep being professional

Do the right things in the right way every day. Try tackling the exercise on this theme called *Professionalism.* Describe the specific things you can do to be super-professional in your work. For example, clarify the customer's goals, make clear contracts, return customer emails promptly, be on time for meetings and fulfil your promises. Follow the daily disciplines to ensure you will always quickly get to 8/10.

Deliver great customer service. Recall a times when you received good service, for example, when visiting a shop, staying in a hotel or buying a product. What did they do right to make you feel special? Great service-givers make you feel welcome, clarify your agenda, explain the options, give you a taster, double-check your goals, make clear contracts, deliver an early success, keep you informed, solve problems and deliver the goods – then add that little bit extra. How can you give great service to customers?

Keep being proactive

Great performers stay ahead of the game. They make things happen, rather than let things happen. Try tackling the exercise on this theme called *Staying Proactive: The Green, Amber & Red Zones*. Describe the things that are happening in each of these zones – then how you can tackle these issues.

The Green Zone – the things that are going well

Peak performers apply the same sense of urgency to the issues that are in the Green Zone as to those in the Red. Michael Schumacher may have been leading a Grand Prix by 20 seconds, for example, but applied the same concentration as if he was 20 seconds behind the leader. Great sales people devote more time to their best customers than to their poor customers. Why? They realise it is the best way to get even more sales. Pacesetters capitalise on what is working. They do not wait for a crisis before springing into action. Looking at your personal and professional life, what is going well at the moment? How can you build on these things?

The Amber Zone – the things that are going okay, but there may be warning signs

"My health may be becoming an issue," said one 35-year old. "During the past year I have put on 2 kilos. Doesn't sound much, but in the old days I was able to lose weight easily. So it's time to start moving. Even though it is January, I am going to start running, rather than wait for the spring."

Looking at your life, what issues are in the Amber Zone? If you manage a team, for example, look out for the warning signs. You may have talented team members who reach 7/10 – then go onto cruise control. Profits may still be on track, but older products are reaching their sell-by date. Team members are losing energy and more people are taking sick leave. Loyal customers call to say they want to stay with you, but are worried about falling service levels. How can you tackle the issues that are in the Amber Zone?

The Red Zone – the things that are going badly or where you experience real pressure

What issues are in this zone? Results may have plummeted at work. Setback follows setback. Key people say they are leaving. The products you offer are out of date. Customers say: "We are looking elsewhere." Suddenly you face a turnaround situation. How can you tackle the issues in the Red Zone?

Peak performers take action early. Looking at the things in the Green Zone, they say: "I must build on this success. If I don't, it may slip into the Amber and then into the Red. I must act now to stay ahead of the game." And, because they are proactive, they spend much of their life in the Green Zone. "Capitalise on what is working and spot the danger signs early," is their motto. Continually tackle issues that are in the Green, Amber and Red Zones.

Gillian Kent is somebody who does superb work. She won the private sector Woman in Technology award in 2005. A former MD of MSN UK, she leads creative teams in which people do three things. 1) They achieve the bottom-line. 2) They combine their talents to do superb work. 3) They successfully manage their life-work balance. The mother of two growing children, she believes strongly in designing a modern work place fit for professionals in the 21st century. MSN UK grew massively, introduced ground-breaking initiatives in child safety and won national awards for improving their employees' 'work-life balance'. "Many people know the 'rules' for running a business," says Gillian, "but the hard part is following these on a daily basis." She describes her rules in the piece called *Running A Successful Business*.

Peak performers love working hard – providing it is the right kind of 'sweat'. They also love helping their customers to succeed. Sometimes they encounter difficulties on the journey, of course, which takes us to the next step.

Running A Successful Business
Gillian Kent

Many people know the rules for running a successful business, but the art is following them every day. The guidelines I follow are:

1)   Know your market.

Know your customer, your competitors and your unique proposition. Wherever possible, do transformational work that has an impact on improving the quality of people's lives.

2)   Set Crystal Clear Goals.

Be ambitious and aim high. Set big, exciting but realistic goals. Dare to focus. Businesses have endless possibilities and choices, with limited resources. There will be many ideas, but you need to prioritise and keep your focus. Make sure that everybody knows what success looks like. They need to know that what they will be doing will make a positive difference.

3)   Keep things simple.

Set a clear, simple strategy. Make sure you are doing the right things in the right order in the right way. Make sure everybody knows their part in implementing the strategy. There is a good test. Walk into any business and ask people to describe: a)The company's goal; b) Their part in making it happen; c) How far the company is towards achieving the goal. Three 'ticks' will tell you the company is probably working as one team towards a common goal.

4)   Build a first class delivery team.

Build a team of people you trust and who you know will deliver. Encourage them to build on their strengths and provide them with the tools to do the job. Pay attention to the 'psychological contract'. Modern professionals are willing to give their best to a company, but also want opportunities to develop. Hire motivated people who will deliver on their promises, but also provide the best possible support and training. Accept that you may be acting as an 'incubator' and people may move-on – so build a queue of people who want to join your company.

5)   Deliver.

Deliver success. Know what is going on. Reality checks are crucial. Keep track of progress and people. Build on what is working, ditch what is not and, most of all, do this quickly. There are always distractions that can throw you off track. Providing you follow these rules, however, the team has a good chance of success.

b) You can find solutions

Every odyssey brings challenges. Sometimes you hear a person say: "Looking back, I am not sure if I would have set-out on the journey if I had known about the difficulties, but I really grew from solving the problems." Great workers continually rehearse potential scenarios – but there are always surprises, which is part of the fun. This section explores three aspects of problem-solving. First, how to find solutions. Second, how to overcome setbacks. Third, how to get support on the journey. Let's explore these topics.

You can use the Five C Model for finding creative solutions

During the early 1990s I was invited to introduce a mentoring programme into Air Miles. The brief was: 'We want to educate our leaders to be good mentors. Give us a framework they can use to pass on their knowledge and also help people to make good quality decisions." The framework should encourage each mentor to express their personality and also be understood by the mentees.

So I based the approach on the Five C Model for creative problem-solving. The mentor could help the person to focus on their challenges, choices, consequences, creative solutions and conclusions. Trying to cut through the mystique, we reframed mentoring as: 'The art of creative problem-solving in a mentoring situation.' (There are many illustrations of how this works in *The Art of Mentoring*.) The Five C Model became the basis for mentoring in organisations such as Air Miles, Microsoft and Sony. Let's explore how this creative problem-solving approach can be used to tackle issues you encounter on your journey.

1) Challenges

Start by defining the challenge. For example: "How can I take the next step in my career? How can I build a successful team? How can I stay calm, rather than get angry?" Clarity is crucial. The key question is: "What are the real results I want to achieve?"

Dare to spend time on this step. For example, one leader asked: "How can I motivate a difficult person in my team?" So I asked, "What are the real results you want to achieve?" Going deeper as he explored the question on various levels, he answered: "I want to learn how to influence the person...I want him to become more positive...I want him to make his best contribution to the team...I want a team of motivated people....I want to build a successful team." So what was the real 'What'? He wanted to build a successful team. The 'How's' for achieving that goal would be very different from those for tackling the first question he posed. Clarify the real 'What' before moving onto the 'How'.

2) Choices

Clarify your choices for tackling the challenge. For example, "Option 'A' is to............Option 'B' is to.........Option 'C' is to........." Keep going until you feel you have brainstormed all the possible options. Don't make any value judgements yet – that is the next step.

3) Consequences

Clarify the consequences of each option. Describe the pluses and minuses of Option 'A', Option 'B', Option 'C', etc. If you wish, rate the attractiveness of each option on a scale 0 – 10. At this point, your head may be full of ideas, so take time-out to reflect.

4) Creative Solutions

Explore the creative solutions. For example, ask yourself: "What are the best parts of each option? Can these be combined into a new option? Looking at the real results to achieve, what has worked before – both for me and for other people? How can I follow those principles in this situation? Are there any other creative solutions?" Keep exploring until you begin settling on a solution and feel ready to move onto the final part.

Creative Problem-Solving:

The Five C Model

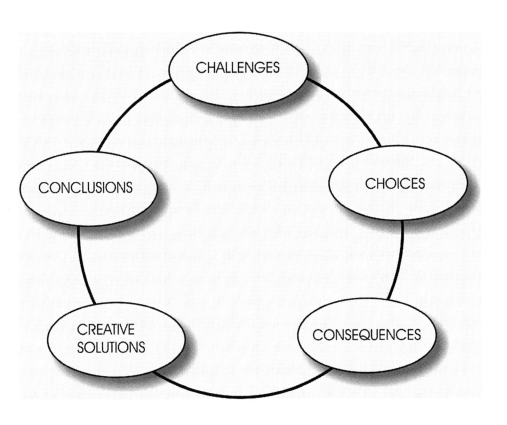

5) Conclusions

Clarify your preferred option. Looking at the real results you want to achieve, which route – or routes – do you want to pursue? (Sometimes you may want to pursue parallel options.) What are the three key things you can do to give yourself the greatest chance of success? How can you maximize the pluses and minimize the minuses? What is your back-up plan? Start working and get an early success.

People can use the Five C Model to take a helicopter view, reflect on the real results they want to achieve and settle on their chosen strategies. Even if they get it right, however, they will sometimes hit the buffers – which takes us to the next tool.

You can overcome setbacks

Everybody meets difficulties in life. Sometimes these are mere irritants, such as your e-mail going down; sometimes they are far more serious. Seeing things in perspective, we realize what is really important in life. Steve Morris and his wife Christine experienced such a life-changing event when they ran the London Marathon in 2003. Christine suffered a stroke and brain hemorrhage. You can read about what happened in the piece called *There's Nothing Like A Setback.*

Two years later they felt ready to emerge into a new world. Looking back, Steve reflects: "When we'd got over the shock, we started to talk about what mattered to us. Family came first, especially our two children. Money came a long way down that list, but then it always did. We certainly sorted out some hefty life insurance. We talked about how we could stay healthy. We decided to take plenty of breaks. We've endlessly discussed how to make our work more meaningful. Above all we tackled some important questions: What are we good at? What do we like doing? How could we do more of both?"

There's Nothing Like A Setback...

Steve Morris

There's nothing like a setback......to really shake us up. And this weekend really does bring back some very resonant memories. Two years ago midway through the London Marathon I received a call on my mobile. It was my wife, or at least it sounded a bit like her. She'd trained for months and this was her first marathon. She was fit and I was waiting near the finish line for her to sail past.

But she didn't sail past and when I heard her voice on the phone, I was filled with certain dread. She was slurred and a bit incoherent. She managed to tell me that she had collapsed and was at a St John's ambulance post somewhere in docklands.

And that was when the nightmare started.

It took me a frantic hour to find her. And over the weeks that followed everything unravelled. It turned out she'd had a brain haemorrhage and a stroke. She was terribly unwell and the medical profession conspired to make everything all the more trying – including one neurologist who told me she was an irrational female who was over anxious (but then he hadn't looked at her MRI scan).

With two daughters aged six and four it certainly was tough for all of us. And Christine and I ran our small business together, so there was strain there too. Our life just came apart.

So that was that. An everyday story of near disaster and the legacy of how to cope and stitch lives back together again.

Well it was tough going, but somehow you switch into a different mode. You do what you need to and keep going. I think it is amazing the way that the urge to make things right beats like a vast drum. You take each day. You go to work. You manage the children and try to keep their fear at bay. You try to offer hope to your loved one and you value those who stick with you well past the original sympathy. But somehow everything is different. Everything uncertain.

Two years on and Christine is well again. We finally found a fantastic consultant who had seen this "runners' condition" before and could help with the recovery. We discovered that Christine also had a heart condition that had contributed to events.

We managed our fear. It took us 18 moths just to talk about it. We focussed on what was important – our children, us. We drew strength from our Church and the incredible support we got.

And then imperceptibly, things started to improve.

I stopped dreaming of ambulances and sirens. I felt a bit more sociable (during the worst of it, I didn't want to do light chat with anyone). I could more calmly drive past the road in Ealing where Christine had collapsed coming home after a procedure on her brain. We started to laugh again. We took small steps. A first break. A half week back at work. My first night out on my own with some friends, eighteen months after the event (Christine finally convinced me she didn't need watching over 24 hours a day!).

So there you have it. The thing about nasty surprises is that they are just that – nasty surprises.

Do setbacks make you stronger? I hope so. I'm not someone who thinks they suddenly make you a new person (at least they didn't for me). I know they leave a bit of scar tissue. I know that things aren't ever quite the same.

On a concrete level it has led to changes. When we'd got over the shock, we started to talk about what mattered to us. Family came first, especially our two children. Money came a long way down that list, but then it always did. We certainly sorted out some hefty life insurance. We talked about how we could stay healthy. We decided to take plenty of breaks. We've endlessly discussed how to make our work more meaningful.

Above all we tackled some important questions:

- *What are we good at?*
- *What do we like doing?*
- *How could we do more of both?*

Christine can't run any more marathons but she is refereeing netball tournaments and doing Tai Chi every week. She's good at sport, she loves doing it and she likes working with youngsters.

I love writing and I like music. I've published a children's book (Noreen the Naughty Troll, available from Amazon). I've taken up the guitar in an attempt to rediscover those old punk glory days! We both love watching cycling having read Lance Armstrong's book.

We decided life was too short to mess about. So we sold our second home in Brighton because the travelling was getting to us. We decided to make one good life in London rather than two compromised ones.

We count our blessings. God gave us gifts and by and large we've used them. We live in a very civilized country. We aren't short of money. We really like our children. We've got some brilliant friends.

On a nice sunny morning, when we are all together as a family I am very glad to be alive. I thank the Lord that the Marathon of 2003 is just a start and not an ending.

Christine and Steve made crucial decisions – and now look back on the marathon as a key turning point in their lives. People react differently after experiencing shocks – but here are three ideas for managing setbacks successfully.

Recognise the stages that people often go through after experiencing a setback.

People may go through the Reactive Change Curve. They travel through Shock; Denial; Paralysis; Anger and Hurt. Healing takes time. But then they climb through the stages of New Strength; New Goals; Hard Work; Success and, eventually, Self-Confidence. People may take time to recover, but they can emerge stronger, wiser and more able to shape their future. (You can discover much more about these stages in the pioneering work done by writers such as Barrie Hopson, Mike Scally and Elisabeth Kubler-Ross.)

Recognise the principles you have followed – and can follow in the future – to manage setbacks successfully.

Try tackling the later exercise called *Managing Setbacks Successfully.* First, looking back on your life, describe a time when you overcame a difficulty. Second, describe what you did right then. Third, describe how you can follow similar principles when faced by difficulties in the future.

Recognise the importance of spending time in a sanctuary, shaping your future and then getting a success.

People who experience setbacks may need to spend time in a 'sanctuary'. They need to make sense of what has happened. Sometimes they simply need to lick their wounds. Give yourself 'permission' to take time-out to relax, re-centre and refocus. You can then move onto shaping your future. Concentrate on what you can control, rather than worry about what you can't. Set specific goals, work hard and get an early success.

The Reactive Change Curve

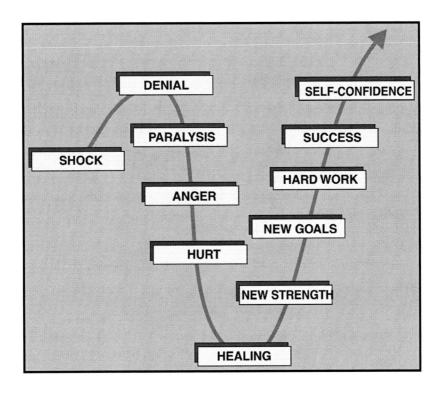

Clive Francis has also recovered from a setback. "I began my cartooning career in 1956, at the age of four," he says. His parents were very proud of the countless scribbles on the backs of old cornflake packets and bare plastered walls of their council house in Hertfordshire. After failing the 11+, he carved a niche as the secondary school cartoonist, leading to his art teacher pointing him in the direction of graphic design. After many varied roles, Clive became 'Cartoonist and Audio Visual Designer' at CWA in Leicester. His work included 16 years of producing the Floyd cartoon strip for Practical Fishkeeping magazine and also Yorky for Volvo Trucks. Life was good but then, in 2004, he received a shock at work. Employing the media that he knows best, Clive describes how he dealt with the setback in the piece called *The R Word: My 52 Step Guide.*

Setbacks can act as alarm calls. Looking back with the benefit of hindsight, sometimes a person says: "On reflection, it was the best thing that ever happened to me." Gathering wisdom from the experience, they use it as a springboard for achieving ongoing success. Let's move on to the next stage.

The 'R' Word: My 52 Step Guide

1. Over 20 years man and boy with the same marketing and design company.

2. Employed as cartoonist/graphic designer.

3. Recently celebrated birthday No. 52.

4. Loyal friend and Managing Director retires.

5. 'New boy' arrives and takes over the business.

6. Shiny shoes and spiky hair, must be good?

7. The writing is on the wall.

8. Company policies suddenly change.

9. Work different, not a cartoon in sight.

10. Phone doesn't ring.

11. Boring…boring!

12. Computer games. Wax legs. Do nails.

13. Going mad.

14. *What a waste of time.*

15. *Depressed.*

16. *Over 20 years with the same company, feeling useless and old.*

17. *Still getting paid though!*

18. *The writing on the wall has a neon glow around it.*

19. *Phone rings at last; it's the 'boy' with shiny shoes.*

20. *Invitation for a chat and a cup of tea.*

21. *I bring the biscuits.*

22. *This must be it?*

23. *Deep breath.*

24. *Informal meeting with a formal edge.*

25. *Due process. Can't mention the 'R' word.*

26. *Perhaps it's time for a change? What are my thoughts?*

27. *What are my bloody options?*

28. *Maybe the field that it is suggested I should be put out in has grass that could be a little greener?*

29. *No one has yet mentioned the 'R' word.*

30. *Handed a sheet of paper explaining what the meeting was about and a date for another in four weeks time.*

31. *Prepare feedback. Do my homework. Financial entitlement?*

32. *Four weeks later. Kind of excited. Escape tunnel is near completion. Is this it?*

33. *Preparing for the inevitable. Be strong. Love change. Take 'The Brave Pill'.*

34. *Deal on the table. Four weeks to consider. Pound signs discussed. 'R' word in print but still not to be mentioned. Due process. Sensitive. Handle with care.*

35. *Excited. More homework. Prepare and plan for the inevitable.*

36. *Inform wife she is soon to be new 'breadwinner'.*

37. *Good job solicitor in wings. Divorce almost on the cards.*

38. *Go out for meal. Discuss the future. Take the plunge. I needed the push anyway. For the best.*

39. *Decision made. Wife happy, although a tad apprehensive.*

40. *Why not up the anti. Nothing to lose?*

41. *Meeting No.3. Papers are signed. Hands shaken. Solicitors sorted. Dates fixed.*

42. *The 'boy' is happy. I am happy. Wife happy. Stomach in turmoil.*

43. *The writing on the wall is now firmly set in stone.*

44. *New 'career' starts in May.*

45. *I shall embrace the 'R' word.*

46. *Time to journey to the world of Freelance before the barriers finally come down.*

47. *Passport being prepared. Tickets on their way. Bags are packed.*

48. *Bags are packed.*

49. *Time for another 'Brave Pill'.*

50. *So what is this **'R'** word I keep talking about?*

51. *It's RESTART of course...what else could it possibly be?*

52. *Looking for my first 3 customers...er: "Hello, is there anybody out there? New kid on the block here!"*

You can get support

Peak performers are resilient – but they also need encouragement. Encouraging other people is incredibly rewarding, but sometimes you can find yourself 'running on empty'. Here are several ways to get help on the journey.

Start by getting the support needed to succeed

Let's explore how to get the support required to do a job. Imagine you are applying for a role in an organisation. Looking at the role, rate the chances of success. Do this on a scale 0 – 10. Anything less than 7 is a danger signal. Even if it is 7+, clarify what must be done to get it nearer to 10/10. Let's assume you go for the interview. Your first job is to establish credibility – but also focus on results, rules and resources. Establish credibility by showing the sponsors you understand their picture of success. Reassure them you will deliver results. Get them across the emotional line where they want to 'buy' you. Once they want to hire you, begin discussing the 'rules – such as the Dos and Don'ts for working well in the organisation. Reassure the sponsors again that you will produce the goods – then move on to resources. Keep showing that you will deliver success, but get the necessary support.

"Sounds reasonable, but what happens if they later try to change the contract?" somebody may ask. Unfortunately, some organisations take this route – which is why you must keep building your network. Security is to always have an alternative. If the contract gets changed, be professional and explain the options to the sponsors:

"There are several ways we can go forward at this point: a) We can follow the agreed route with the required support. The pluses are these....The minuses are these....b) We can try to do the project with half the support. The pluses are these....The minuses are these....c) We can choose not to do it. The pluses are these....The minuses are these....There may also be several other possibilities. Bearing these options in mind, which route do you want us to follow?"

Be calm. Do not back the sponsors into a corner. Be prepared to look for 'win-wins'. After outlining the options, you will find that they often provide support. If it is not forthcoming, buy time. Reflect on the discussion and settle on your chosen way forward. If necessary, be prepared to walk. Sounds a difficult process? Perhaps, but do not choose to be a victim. Do whatever is possible to set-up the project to succeed.

Spend time with Encouragers

Spend time with encouragers, rather than stoppers. Try tackling the later exercise called *My Self-Confidence Pot,* which was devised by Virginia Satir, a great family therapist. (I included this in *The Magic of Work.* So many people found Virginia's exercise useful, however, that I have included it here too.) Start by drawing an imaginary pot (see illustration.) Then go through the following steps.

• Looking at the pot, draw a line that corresponds with how high you feel your self-confidence is today. If you have high confidence, draw it high up the pot. If your confidence is low, draw the line at a lower point in the pot. Now let's consider why it may be at this level.

• Write the names of the 'Pot Fillers': the people in your life who put encouragement and energy into your pot. Similarly, write the things you do to encourage yourself or put energy into your pot. If you get lots of encouragement, 'your cup will runneth over', and you are more likely to encourage other people. But there may be complications, which brings us to the next part of the exercise.

My Self-Confidence Pot

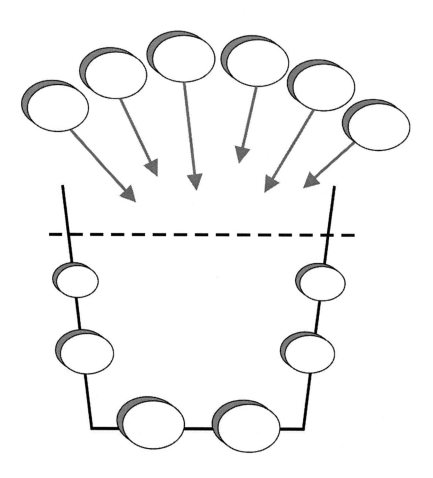

- Write the names of the 'Pot Drillers': the Discouragers and Energy Drainers. The more significant they are in your life, the nearer they will be to the base. Also, can you think of any ways that you might drill holes in your own pot? One other point: some people may be both Pot Fillers and Pot Drillers. Sometimes they may be helpful, but other times they may be hurtful. Clarify the specific things they do to support or stop you.

How to use this information? Encouragement may flow in the top of the pot but, if there are holes in the bottom, it will drain away. You will have a daily struggle to maintain the same level of confidence. So what are the solutions?

1) *Spend more time with people who give you energy.*
   Start by spending time with your Encouragers. If possible, only work with colleagues you find stimulating. People often find that, as they get older, they spend more time with personal and professional soul mates. Encourage yourself. Do more of the things you love, for example, listening to music, skiing, visiting the theatre or whatever. Pursuing these activities will put more energy into your pot.

2) *Spend less time – or no time – with people who drain energy.*
   Radical changes are difficult to make overnight but, unless the holes are filled, encouragement will simply flow out of the bottom. You can do two things with the stoppers.

Stop seeing people who drain energy

Why take such a drastic step? Energy is life. You need pure energy, rather than poisonous energy. Radical changes are difficult to make overnight but, unless the holes are filled, encouragement will simply flow out of the bottom. For example, two of the main reasons why people leave their jobs are: a) They are working for a manager who makes life difficult each day; b) They are doing work that no longer gives them a sense of fulfilment. So they begin searching for satisfying work with a manager whom they respect.

Start making clear contracts with the people who both encourage and stop you

Reward the positive. Give clear messages about the specific things you do like them doing. Explain how you would like to build on these parts of the relationship. Give positive alternatives to the negative. Say: "In the future, is it possible for you to ….." or "I would prefer it if you…" Present suggestions, rather than label them as 'bad'. Don't expect people to respond immediately; everybody needs time to lick their wounds. Don't argue or fall into the blame game. What if the person refuses to respond? Then make the decision whether to stay or leave.

Be an encourager – a pot-filler – for other people

Encourage other people and they are more likely to support you. Give and give – but don't become a victim. Do not stay around to have your pot drilled by people who choose to be miserable or 'observer critics'.

Encourage yourself

Every adventure brings highs and lows. Sometimes you will be travelling across a wilderness – not knowing when you will find the next resting place. So how can you give yourself energy on the journey? Here are some suggestions.

a) **Build-on your successes.**
During the 1970s I began inviting people to keep a daily journal called *My Right Book*. They were asked to describe: 'Three things I have done right today – and how I can do more of these things in the future. Two things I can do even better – and how.' People enjoyed the exercise and, as a by-product, embarked on the process of self-development.

b) **Count your blessings.**
This is an old motto, but still good to remember – especially during times of crisis. Try tackling the exercise on this theme called *My Assets*. After suffering a big financial loss, one person said:

"The setback has been tough, but I need to keep things in perspective. My assets are that I have good health, a fantastic wife, a home, a garden, some money in the bank, my creativity, great clients, enormous drive and the ability to generate an income stream. I can build on these to shape my future."

c) **Build-in time for rest and recovery.**
Climbing any mountain is arduous, so set aside periods for recovery. Apart from re-energising the body, it is important to refresh the mind. Taking time out to re-centre also enables you to make good quality decisions. Some people feel guilty about creating recovery time. Providing you have done your best, however, it is vital to recharge your batteries. Try tackling the later exercise on this theme called *Results Require Proper Rest & Recovery.* Build-in periods when you can regain your strength. You will then be more alert and on top of your game.

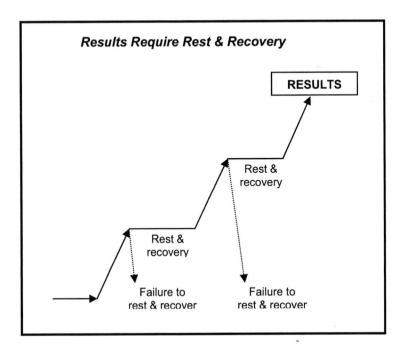

d) **Make good use of the 'fallow times'.**
Peak performers love to experience a sense of flow. When doing a rewarding project, for example, they really get into the groove. But after completing the job, they sometimes go into the doldrums, as if they have lost their sense of purpose. Here are some suggestions for making good use of the time in-between projects.

- *Recognise the importance of the fallow times.*
  Finishing is great – but can also lead to a feeling of anti-climax. After experiencing flow, you may go to the other extreme and feel frustrated. Sometimes people get impatient and jump into the next project, even though it is not too stimulating. During this phase it is useful to remember the agricultural tradition of allowing a field to lie fallow. The field can then rest, recover and be revitalised. Creative artists know the value of 'giving themselves permission' to be fallow. Providing they use such times properly, they can relax, re-centre and refocus. Fallow times can be fruitful times. They are vital for revitalisation.

- *Recognise how to use the fallow times.*
  "During the fallow times I surround myself with positive things," said one person. "Getting up in the morning, I play my favourite music. This provides a stimulating start to the day, rather than listening to politicians arguing on the radio. I spend time with friends who give me energy, rather than negative people. 'Everything is food', say the Zen Buddhists, so I control what I allow into my body. Because I am in a vacuum, I must set the agenda – even if it means choosing to 'do nothing' – rather than allow others to set the agenda. Surrounding

myself with positive influences means I am eventually more likely to find a meaningful purpose."

Are you prepared to give yourself permission to be fallow? If so, for how long? It may be okay to continue working at your 'day job', for example, whilst gathering information about future challenges. How can you surround yourself with positive things during this time? How will you know when to move onto the next project? If you wish, try tackling the later exercise on this theme called *The Fallow Times.*

- *Recognise when it is time to move out of being fallow and go into flow*
  Providing you do the right things, eventually a stimulating 'project' will emerge. Consider whether it fits with your personal or professional goals. If it does, seize the opportunity. If it doesn't, but you are tempted to spring back into action, make sure it is a challenge you respect. Otherwise, like a mountaineer who does not respect the mountain, you may suffer catastrophe. Making good use of the fallow times means you are more likely to choose the right project.

e)   **Build-in time for 'slow thinking'.**
Carl Honore, the author of *In Praise of Slow,* believes in getting the right balance between fast thinking and slow thinking. Fast thinking generates the pieces of the jigsaw – but slow thinking is needed to make sense of the whole picture. Many of our epiphanies arrive when we give ourselves time to reflect. Here are three suggestions you may wish to consider.

- *Create time in the day to do some slow thinking.*
  This is challenging – especially in the business world of back-to-back meetings. Start the day by taking time to look ahead. Rehearse the many different scenarios and your potential strategies. Before going into a meeting, focus on the real results to achieve – then be fully present in the session. Schedule meetings to take 45

minutes, rather than 1 hour. You will get more done – but also have time to make sense of the last meeting and prepare for the next. Balance time spent in your 'cave' and around the 'campfire'. Open plan offices are notorious for interruptions. If you want to write, find a good 'cave' – then visit the 'camp fire' for meetings. Walk outside in the fresh air for 15 minutes. You will get oxygen, stimulate your brain and gain perspective – which are all needed to make good quality decisions.

- *Create time in your life to do some slow thinking.*
  This can also be challenging – especially if you have children – because the weekends fly by. Plan your time in blocks. If possible, work from home on Friday. Getting your life in perspective can be helped by taking a long weekend – perhaps going away with your partner. The first day will be spent winding-down, the final day preparing for the week ahead, but you will get some quality time in-between. When exploring a topic, start by focusing on the big picture. Clarify the 'What' – the real results you want to achieve – before moving to the 'How'. Focus on what is important in life. Clarifying your real priorities helps to make good decisions.

- *Create time for your team to do some slow thinking.*
  Great teams set aside time for 'slowing thinking'. Sounds crazy? Perhaps, but one super team I know devote 3 days a year to this activity. Many teams have 'away days' – but this team's 'slow thinking' days are done in the spirit of exploration. They explore topics, really listen to each other and then find creative solutions. Creativity is often about the process of 'opening up' – clarifying the result to achieve and exploring ideas – then 'closing down'. Business meetings can have a culture of closing-down the discussion before people have defined the real 'What'. People leap into action and climb a mountain, but it may be the wrong one. Great teams get the right balance

between opening-up and closing-down. They focus on strategy – then tactics – and do superb work.

- *Spend time in your sanctuary*
  Where do you feel at peace? Where do you go to make sense of the world? Everybody needs a place where they can relax, re-centre and refocus. Try tackling the exercise called *My Sanctuaries.* Perhaps you have a favourite place in your garden; like to walk in the woods; or visit particular soul mates. Spending time in sanctuaries offers the chance to rise above daily tasks. You can then make good decisions about shaping your future.
  People who get encouragement – and who encourage themselves – are more likely to move onto the next step, which is probably what we are here to do.

c) *You can help other people to succeed*

The Strengths Way has an underlying theme: "How can we use our strengths to help others to succeed?" Everybody has different talents, everybody can serve in different ways – what is your way? Alec Dickson, the founder of Voluntary Service Overseas and Community Service Volunteers, inspired many people to give to others. He explained the birth of these two organisations by saying:

"We needed to tap into people's desire to build a better world. For example, I saw that young people had enormous idealism and, at the same time, there were many unmet needs in society. So why not match these two together? We could use the young people's energy to meet those needs and build a better world."

There are many ways to give. Some people give economically, some give emotionally, some give in an educational way – but encouragement is at the heart of all giving. We want to help others to enjoy health, hope and happiness. Alec Dickson believed that the giver often received as much as the receiver. Why? Our self fades into the background when we are giving – yet we often feel more real afterwards. What is your preferred way of giving? Let's look at somebody who has a unique way of passing-on her knowledge.

Kelly Marks is one of the country's leading experts in horse psychology. Previously a leading jockey and show jumper, she now works with troubled horses. She finds solutions that benefit both the horses and their owners – but I have also seen her in action as an outstanding coach. Kelly's first love has always been working with horses – but she also pioneered sessions showing people how they could apply certain communication principles.

During the past decade I have taken several teams to work with Kelly. People enjoyed the individual sessions in which they each did a 'join-up' with a horse. Within five minutes they got a new horse to walk beside them around a ring and follow their instructions. The highlight for me, however, was watching Kelly. She gave each person her complete attention. Encouraging and patient, she did whatever was necessary to help them to achieve success. Kelly feels she owes a great deal to her mentor, Monty Roberts. She described her debt to him in the piece called *My Gratitude to a Great Teacher.*

My Gratitude to a Great Teacher

Kelly Marks

In September 1992 I was working with racehorses when a visiting lady asked if we wanted to see this 'Californian Horse Psychologist'. A 'what'?! Having missed any previous hype about Monty, I had no preconceptions when my father and I went to a small indoor school near Newbury. Sitting on straw bales, we waited to see what it was all about. No music, nor fanfare – just a short introduction; then we watched this man work with two different horses. He let the horses run around the pen (individually I hasten to add), then they'd decide to follow him. After he'd put a saddle on their back, they'd buck, but then they came back towards him. After a short spell of being 'long-lined' – moving around the pen on a long line – they were happy to be ridden. Weird. Normally it took people several weeks to ride such horses – and he did it in half-an-hour.

Several weeks later I visited the yard where Monty was working, aiming to gather more knowledge. Watching him in action, my feeling was, 'This guy is smart alright – but so are a lot of the old horsemen and dealers. He's definitely worth watching, but is it anything special?' I didn't get to speak with Monty on these occasions, but someone bought him to our house one day while I was out. He got to meet my dog, Willoughby, which was to prove an important meeting.

When the Student is Ready,
the Teacher Will Appear

Flash forward to May 1993. I volunteered to take 15 students in their early 20's for 10 days in France for a horsey study trip. Some extra-keen students and I had got up early to meet a race horse trainer, who had promised to show us some especially beautiful training grounds. We sat in a mini-bus, parked in a garage at 7.15 a.m., the time we had arranged to meet the trainer. Then someone pulled-up right behind us.

My dear students, who occasionally enjoyed 'winding me up', shouted: 'There's this big French farmer coming up to your window and he's furious you've parked in his way!' I gave up trying to escape as I stalled the minibus for the second time and was ready to apologise to the man at the window. Who should it be? Not an angry farmer at all, but Monty Roberts. His first words to me were: 'You're the girl with the wonderful dog aren't you?' It was at that moment I realised this man was indeed someone special –a man of intelligence – with great taste in dogs!

We had come to meet through that experience common in foreign speaking countries–meeting someone who speaks the same language. They become your 'New Best Friend'. Certainly this was the case with Monty who, having been in France and speaking with virtually nobody in the previous two weeks. He said it was like Christmas and his Birthday had come at the same time when he saw the English writing on the side of the minibus! Monty immediately offered to take all the mini-bus gang for a beer and talk at his hotel that afternoon. Gratefully accepting his invitation, we were all with him for over 3 hours. The students – a sometimes rowdy bunch – were the quietest they'd been on the whole trip. Talking with Monty at the end, he told me about a book he's been trying to put together for over 8 years. He gathered that I loved books and writing as well, so he asked if I'd be able to help him when he next came to England. So that's where it all started.

Monty came to England a month later and, on June 16, he gave me his manuscript. In addition to working on the book, I also helped with the 'remedial' horses he was working with on his visit. Two other helpers where Richard 'Max' Maxwell, who is now a well-known trainer in his own right, and Tim Piper, who is making a success of running a stud in the West Country. Working with the horses, we'd all start at 8 am in the morning and continue right through to the early evenings. I love what I'm doing now, but still look back at that summer with great fondness and as one of the best times of my life.

Previously I'd worked with good horse people who emphasised seeing events from the horse's point of view. That summer was extra special, however, because we were encouraged to share our own ideas – and our opinions were respected. Maybe this sounds archaic to today's young people but, at the time, being a woman in racing had an air of invisibility. Maybe it had nothing to do with being female. The tradition was 'he who pays says', but this meant that bosses missed-out on lots of valuable information. That summer taught me the value and fun of having someone actually listen. Getting people to respect their own ideas is something I work at developing, particularly on our Horse Psychology 'problem solving' weekends. It's still quite foreign to many people. I tell them: "Just because something is your idea and not something you've been told or you've read in a book first, doesn't mean it's not brilliant!"

Give a Man a Fish and You Feed Him for a Day. Teach Him to Fish And....

Monty taught me many lessons about horses that summer – such as having a positive attitude and the power of focus. He may be a genius, but sometimes things go wrong. But his positive attitude made the difference, carrying him through to help 'lost causes' of the horse world. Faced by a seemingly insurmountable problem – such as a frightened horse that had been mistreated for years – he somehow 'knew' he was going to find the way forward. Setbacks were just that – setbacks and not disasters. He would not lose a beat and kept working to resolve the situation. This seems a great attitude to have, not just when working with horses; but for life in general.

Monty's positive attitude gave the impression that he could constantly 'pull rabbits out of hats'. An illustration came when I accompanied him on demonstration tours in England and Ireland. "This is not meant to happen," I said to myself, watching him trying to fasten the girth on a 'remedial' horse that was making serious attempts to kick his head off. His brain was ticking away, then he said: "Kelly, in my equipment bag there is that really old, stiff leather hobble (stirrup leather). Can you just throw that in please?" As he doubled it over and reached under the horse, ignoring the back foot taking well kicks, he was able to gently bring the girth under the stomach and fasten it on the saddle. Creative thinking is a muscle that can be built. So often we can limit ourselves to narrow frames of reference – losing out on flashes of the blindingly obvious. Sometimes when it comes to 'but this isn't in the script' there can be a tendency to freeze, not acknowledging just how ingenious we are all capable of being.

So what have I learned from Monty? Mention his name to people and you will get many different reactions. Some mention 'join-up', others say 'The Horse Whisperer', believing he wrote that book, rather than *his own, 'The Man Who Listens To Horses'. Some people still see him as controversial; even through his methods have been adopted by some of the most die-hard horse trainers. Others talk about his work for the Queen or how his ideas can be used in school. The most important gift Monty has given me, however, is a way forward, a way to think things out for myself.*

I don't know if Monty has ever studied Chinese philosophers. If he has, he may take some consolation from the words of Lao Tzu. "The Wise Leader, when his task is accomplished, his work done, throughout the country everyone says 'It happened of its own accord'." Many people are becoming more sympathetic and respectful in their treatment of horses. People are making far more attempt to see things from the horses' point of view. Maybe it was going to happen of its own accord. Maybe it has a great deal to do with a man called Monty Roberts.

You can be an encourager

Perhaps I was fortunate when I began working with people. Because I had no formal 'training', I asked virtually everybody I met: "What has helped you to grow most in your life?" One key theme came through loud and clear.

"I had somebody who encouraged me. My grandma...my teacher...my friend...my housefather at the children's home. They were loving but tough. Because they told me what I did right, I was more ready to listen when I did something wrong. They made me feel as if I was the most important person in the world."

So it seemed obvious to focus on encouragement and, fortunately, the young people responded to this approach. Good encouragers are like great educators. They focus on the three E's: Encouragement, Enterprise and Excellence. Let's explore these themes.

Encouragement

Try tackling the exercise called *Being An Encourager.* Looking back on your life, write the names of three people who have encouraged you. For example, a parent, teacher, sports coach, manager, friend, child, writer, artist or whoever. What did they do right to encourage you? How can you follow these principles in your own way to encourage other people? (People are different, of course, and may want different kinds of encouragement. So it is vital to check with individuals how they want to be supported.)

Enterprise

"Look for when people 'come alive'," said George Lyward, one of my teachers. "Look for when they 'reach out' to learn something new or do creative work. Dare to say what you see them doing right. Sometimes they may brush it off by saying, 'It is nothing.' But dare to tell them anyway, they will remember it for a long time." Good encouragers are like talent spotters. They look for when somebody shows initiative and reward this sense of enterprise.

Excellence

Great coaches in sport, for example, work together with an athlete to help them to achieve excellence. You won't necessarily do that with people in your personal life – sometimes giving encouragement is enough. But if you are a manager, for instance, you can educate and enable committed people to achieve excellence. Encouragement is the foundation and we never forget a good encourager – they stay with us forever.

David Pilbeam is a superb encourager. Beginning his working life as a teacher, he spent five years teaching in International Schools in Malawi and Portugal. He then moved into the hospitality business in Hong Kong. Returning to the UK, he became the Operations Director for a chain of health and leisure clubs. David moved on to working with the Tom Peters Company, specialising in the area of leadership, before co-founding the Talent Network. He also works as a mentor and coach to people in organisations. What has helped him to grow in his life? David recounts the key themes in the piece called *Messages From Mentors.*

Messages From Mentors

David Pilbeam

We all have mentors at various times in our career. I have been fortunate to have worked for, been influenced by, and loved, a few. My professional and private life would look very different without them. Here's my shortlist of learning from a few people who have stretched me over the years – and they still do.

1) Be courageous.

Well, I thought I would start with the easiest! David Maister writes in his book True Professionalism "How often can you repeat the basic advice of "Listen to your clients, provide outstanding service, train your people, look for and eliminate inefficiencies, and act like team players?" The problem, clearly, is not in figuring out what to do. Rather, the problem is to find the strength and courage to do what we know to be right." Many times I have 'sat on' something until the pain got so great that I just had to act. With a bit of courage, I just might have got going on that project sooner.

2) Be there!

Woody Allen once said: "Ninety percent of success is showing up." On a professional level, this means be early for appointments and be prepared. On a personal level, give your full attention to each person. Great facilitators, for example, listen to what a person says, find the themes and enable the person to be more real, more themselves. They can only do that if they are fully present in the moment.

3) Be a talent spotter.

Sure, it's cool to demonstrate mastery yourself. But learning to look for and expose others to the talent of friends and colleagues not only feels great but gets you results as well. Phil Jackson, winning coach of both Chicago Bulls and LA Lakers, once said to Michael Jordan early in his career; 'The sign of a great player is not how much he scores, but how much he lifts his team-mate's performance.' Jordan and the 'Bulls' never looked back. Even the greatest performers revel in the talent of others.

4) **Be real.**

Listen, watch and learn but ultimately you have to be 'YOU' to be credible. Larry Bossidy and Ram Charan get to the heart of this in their book Execution: "Who you are is the same as what you do and say. Only authenticity builds trust, because sooner or later people spot the fakers." Carl Rogers, the humanistic psychologist, explained the need to be 'congruent' – while the existentialists talked about living in either 'good faith' or 'bad faith'. Be true to yourself and help others to be authentic.

5) **See things in perspective.**

"Lighten-up". I got this message (AGAIN!) loud and clear from a wise and trusted source just a few days ago. Most of us take our work seriously – and we must if we are to succeed. But it is vital to keep things in perspective. Compared to most people on the planet, some of us are very privileged. The decisions we take at work are important but, apart from those in the medical profession, do not necessarily involve life and death. The constant search for success can drain us and take-away the real essence of who we are and how we can serve other people. At the same time, we also need encouragement. By all means work hard, but be sure to play hard as well! Don't take yourself too seriously.

You can pass on your knowledge to other people

"Artists try to cheat death by leaving a legacy," we are told. They write a poem, paint a picture, create a symphony, design a building or whatever. Everybody is an artist. Everybody is also a teacher in the way they behave as a person and as a model. Let's explore how you can share your wisdom.

Try tackling the exercise called *Passing-on Knowledge.* Describe the professional and personal know-how you can share with people. The professional side may be relatively easy. Certainly you can pass on strategies, skills and experience in your role as, for example, a manager or coach. The personal side may take more time to formulate. "I am not sure I have anything to offer," somebody may say. So how can you clarify the lessons you have learned in your life?

Try tackling the exercise called *Wise Words.* Imagine that you have been invited to address a group of 18-year-olds. You have been given 10 minutes to give them 3 key messages about principles they may want to follow in their future lives. What would you tell them? Write the 3 key messages you would give. Try to bring each one to life by giving concrete examples. Sometimes I give the *Wise Words* exercise on workshops. It provides a different emphasis and, of course, is a way of getting people to share their life-philosophy. A highly successful MD of high tech company said she would give the following messages:

"1) Do the things you enjoy – especially in your work.

Why? You will be spending at least 9 hours a day in a work place, possibly for the next 40 years. Sound depressing? Not if you are doing what you love. Many of our most famous entrepreneurs started-out by using their enjoyment muscle. Do not ignore money, you must pay your way, but always feed your enjoyment as well as your wallet.

"2) Be kind.

This sounds obvious – but you will meet many situations in life where you can make a choice. Will I be kind or cruel; will I say positive words or negative words; will I help the planet or hurt the planet? So you see, we are talking about big things –

about your relationship with people, your environment and yourself. If you are kind, you will find that you like yourself more during your life.

"3) Stretch yourself.
Be the best you can be. Personally, I have always responded well to setting targets. Because I was good at exams, I aimed to get an 'A'. But people are intelligent in different ways. My 14-old-year old daughter, for example, is interested in drama, rather than academic results. We want her to get reasonable grades, but encourage her to use of her main talent. So last week she set herself some goals in her drama studies. She wants to improve her singing voice and dancing. Whatever your talent, stretch yourself and fulfil your potential."

Everybody wants to leave a legacy. They often want to pass on lessons about what has worked for them in their lives. Or, conversely, what they wished they had experienced. So they aim to create a beautiful childhood for their children; build a new kind of school; invent software that empowers future generations; make money – then invest it in medical research. Artists try to create something that will last forever. But everybody's life makes a difference. Planting positive seeds is more likely to give hope to future generations. What do you want to pass on to people?

The Strengths Way is really about encouragement. Throughout this book we have focused on people who have used their strengths to help others. Starting with a dream, they demonstrated the desire and discipline required to deliver – which takes us to the next step.

d) You can work to achieve success

Let's return to your picture of success – the milestones you want to look back on when you are 80. How far are you along this road? What have you accomplished so far in your life? What do you want to give to people in the next years? Life is about gathering experience, making sense of experience and passing-on experience. "Live, learn, love, labour and leave a legacy," we are told. What will give you a sense of peace? What do you want to be your personal or professional legacy?

Archie Duncanson has achieved some of his aims – which included publishing a ground-breaking book. During the 1980s I met him when he attended a Strengths Building course in Sweden. An American living in that country, he was working as a computer engineer. Although he was good at his job, it was simply a way of earning a living. Over the years, however, he developed another dream. Frustrated by the powerlessness people expressed when talking about the environment, Archie began to take small steps in his own world – steps that eventually led to producing his best-selling book called *Ecology Begins At Home.* He writes:

> "I set about trying to reduce my garbage – and succeeded, step by step! Then I began cutting down my laundry detergent, other chemicals and electricity. I repaired things instead of throwing them away. I bought higher quality: fresh organic vegetables, cloth table napkins instead of paper, and other things that last. My life began feeling it had more quality and yet I saved money and pollution. I was so satisfied with my experiments and results that I wanted to share them with others! But I wasn't ready for a book yet – I lacked the confidence."

Archie eventually embarked on the long journey of writing, illustrating and self-publishing the book. (You can read about journey in the piece called *The Story of Ecology Begins At Home.*) Even though it was written in English, it gained a wide following in Sweden, where it was frequently used in schools and colleges. Aiming to communicate his message to a wider audience, Archie initially failed to get it published in the US and the UK, so he decided to put it on the internet. During the process, however, he was approached by Green Books, who wanted to publish it in the UK. he book sold well and received excellent reviews. *Permaculture Magazine* wrote: "This is definitely the best book yet on how to green your lifestyle." Pointing out that many environmental books made people feel overwhelmed and dispirited, the review continued:

"Archie Duncanson's book is different. It shows how one man looked around him and saw what he could do to reduce his personal ecological footprint. Using the power of choice, he is making his contribution to the environmental effort and inspiring others to do the same. On the basis that you only need to take one step to make a difference, Archie takes you on the first stage of his journey towards a more environmentally friendly home and an easier conscience. With delightful illustrations, and packed full of simple ideas to reduce the ecological impact of your daily life, *Ecology Begins at Home* is an inspiration for adults and children alike."

The Story of
'Ecology Begins At Home'

Archie Duncanson

As a boy I admired many writers and wanted to be like them. One was Thomas Paine who wrote essays on democracy at the time of the American Revolution. I admired him for speaking out for what he believed-in. At the age of 13 I had nothing revolutionary to write about, so I tried to write a short story. I didn't get very far – nothing came!

So I concluded that I wasn't meant to be a writer and gave up. I became an engineer instead and enjoyed being creative in design and analysis. As for writing, when I was far from home I wrote long letters to family and friends, giving a travelogue and sharing my reflections with them. I always enjoyed the writing – it gave me the feeling of having a conversation with a like-minded soul.

The years went by and still I felt I had little special to share, apart from my engineering work with colleagues. Then one day a friend who was part of an amateur poetry circle said they were putting out a little booklet of poetry, and asked if I would I like to do some drawings to illustrate the poems. Despite apprehension and worry about criticism, I decided to give it a go. I had fun using my imagination and coming up with interesting drawings and I got only positive feedback. Thus at age 40 I took my first step out into the public eye.

Discouraged with the World, I Decided to Act

About this time, I became very discouraged with the world's problems, especially the environment, and with what politicians and authorities were doing to solve them. Nothing was happening; the environment was getting worse, not better! Out of this discouragement I one day decided to act and see if I couldn't do something on a very small scale at home in my own little private world.

I set about trying to reduce my garbage – and succeeded, step by step! Then I began cutting down my laundry detergent, other chemicals and electricity. I repaired things instead of throwing them *away. I bought higher quality: fresh organic vegetables, cloth table napkins instead of paper, and other things that last. My life began feeling it had more quality and yet I saved money and pollution. I was so satisfied with my experiments and results that I wanted to share them with others! But I wasn't ready for a book yet. You might be, but I lacked the confidence.*

So I took a smaller step, I wrote a three page letter describing what I was doing, how anybody could do similar things, and how satisfying it was – that we can each affect the big world problems with garbage, chemicals and energy by doing our part at home. I made one hundred copies and sent them out to friends all over the world. Soon I got back many positive replies. Friends liked the ideas and the fact that I had actually done something, rather than just thinking about it. My friend Carol wrote back: "Someone should write a book telling us what to buy, what to eat, etc. for the good of the environment."

My eyes fastened upon the word 'someone' and I thought: I could do that. The more I thought about it, the more I felt I was just the right 'someone'. I had the personal experience, I had the pedagogical skills to explain things simply and I had the desire.

I Decided to Share My Experiences

I put together an outline of the subjects I wanted to include in my little handbook for living 'environmentally friendly' – garbage, chemicals, food, clothes, the car, etc. I kept my list short because my intention was not to write an all inclusive reference book, but to enthuse and inspire into action others who were discouraged as I had been. I simply wanted to say, look, it's easy to solve the world's big problems, just start with your own share at home!

With that purpose I began writing, subject by subject. Instead of talking problems I gave example after example of my solutions. Using my experiences as a teacher drawing on the blackboard, I used simple diagrams, pictures and tables to get the message across straight-away without a lot of words. I kept it simple and made it fun, which was not hard since I myself had experimented with enthusiasm and watched my results grow with joy and satisfaction.

When I went to the library in the 1980's to learn more, I noticed that most of the books on the environment were disheartening. They detailed fully the overwhelming nature of the problems and solutions were described as being dependent on everyone changing their habits ("If everyone would take public transport to work instead of the car...") which seemed unrealistic, if not impossible. Most books were several hundred pages long, filled with small print that made green living seem like a difficult science in which you could make many mistakes if you were not careful. I saw my task as that of a good teacher, to provide the essentials in a given short time, and to make it enjoyable and interesting as well as useful.

With this vision in mind, I had to rewrite some sections of my text again and over again many times until I felt satisfied. The section on the car was the most difficult; I so easily fell into blaming the manufacturers and the oil industry. I had to step back and ask myself: "What had I written that was new and interesting, that added to the positive alternatives and not just to the blame?" I knew that I did not have all the answers, but wanted to share the best of the ones I did have. So my approach to the car was to tell how happy and satisfied I felt every time I saved a litre of petrol by riding my bike or walking to the shops.

When I had a rough draft of the whole book, I showed it to friends. My reviewing friends were both encouraging and helpful in their comments. Out of our discussions came new ideas for solving environmental problems in daily life and new thoughts about how to present the material to beginners. I am grateful still today for all the support that people gave me. Finally, I was done to my own satisfaction. My story was told to the best of my ability and illustrated with my own drawings. I was ready to go to print.

Publishing My Book and Bringing It Home!

It came as a revelation to me that any person anywhere can go to a print shop and, for a fee, pay to have their manuscript printed and bound as a book! In fact, most books throughout history were published privately, until the last century or so, when publishing houses came to dominate! I did not have the confidence to go to a publisher, so instead went to a special place in Stockholm, Writer's

Book Machine (Forfattares Bokmaskin), a nonprofit cooperative print shop where the author prints his or her book cheaply by doing much of the work themselves: layout, mounting, collating, binding, trimming – everything except the actual printing. They were very helpful and I learned how to make a book. When I did the binding, which required handling each copy many times, I felt like an artisan from an earlier century. It strengthened the feeling that my book was a personal gift to each reader as well as to the world.

It is hard to describe the feeling I had when I brought the first printing of 500 copies home. After living with it for a year so intensively, like a pregnancy, here was my ecology book now in my hand! As I looked at it, it almost seemed as if a stranger had produced it, and I could not fully comprehend that I had had the perseverance to handle all the thousand and one details that went into its making. But, like finishing college or running a marathon, I had concentrated on one step at a time, and kept at it until I reached my goal. Like Pooh Bear, I felt very satisfied with myself.

Spreading the Book in the World

I had no publisher to do the selling and advertising, so I sent the book out to magazines and newspapers in Sweden where I lived. I quickly got an excellent review in a popular green magazine, whose editor even offered to help me by selling the book via the magazine. Despite the fact that the book was in English (a foreign language in Sweden), it received many glowing reviews. They liked its simplicity, positive attitude, practicality, and that it offered the reader a chance to make a difference. I was aglow! All my dreams had come true! I had succeeded!

From the magazine articles, people wrote or called me to order the book. I sold it for a low price to encourage its spread and usually sent them off the same day. I began translating the text into Swedish so that it would be in the reader's native language. The Swedish edition came out 4 months later, published at the same place. This time I dared to produce a thousand copies. They sold like hotcakes. After a very fine review in the Swedish Library Journal, virtually every library in the country ordered it, so I went back and this time printed four thousand copies – the binding and trimming wasn't quite as thrilling as the first time, but still very satisfying knowing that every reader, even in a public library, was receiving a personal gift directly from me.

Soon invitations were coming in from schools, communities and environmental organizations to talk about the ideas in the book. I had a lot of fun giving talks and meeting some of my readers and others who thought in the same way as I did. It also gave joy and satisfaction, confirming my belief that people truly want to care for the planet – they just need to know that what they do makes a difference – and a little basic info on how to make better choices. I loved telling about my many composting failures (before I got it right) and demonstrating how to cook spaghetti and pasta without extra water, saving half or more of the cooking energy. I showed slides from my home experiments and displayed gadgets that I had made.

I summarised my message with a one page handout titled "Archie's Eco-Checklist", which gave examples from my actions in the areas of garbage, chemicals, energy and food for the reader to check-off when they had tried them. Within a year the book and its ideas were all over Sweden, spreading the joy and satisfaction of personal environmental responsibility to homes, day care centres and schools.

I also sent the book to international environmental organisations and to magazines in America, but with no response at all. With a slight touch of bravado, I sent it off in 1989 to President Ronald Reagan, Soviet Premier Michael Gorbatjov, several European heads of state, Prince Charles of Britain and to the King of Sweden!

The book spread slowly in other countries through friends abroad and readers with international contacts. Due to the difficulty of selling internationally, I decided to send out free copies whenever requests came in. Over the years I sent out more than a thousand free copies of the English edition to interested individuals around the world. Some wrote back describing their use of the book in environmental education, which was satisfying for me. My address was in the back of the book, and I made many interesting acquaintances through this work.

In the U.S., I printed a separate edition and with the help of my sisters and friends sold about 500 copies but eventually gave away the rest. Without my presence and without distribution channels, the book never took off as it had in Sweden. In my innocence I relied on individuals and NGOs to help me spread the book with its ideas, as had happened in Sweden. I had hoped environmental organisations would sponsor cheap translations and local non-commercial editions in different countries. Stubbornly, I refused all offers for commercial editions and so lost many possible translations, with all of their potential readers.

After six years of working with the book in Sweden, demand abruptly died off in 1997 and I had to look for other work. That was OK, because it had done its job in Sweden and I was ready for a change. But I was not quite satisfied because I still had many copies in English in my cellar and it had never gotten off the ground outside of Sweden. As I took up other employment, I decided to give all remaining copies to libraries and schools. I began sending them out to universities and public libraries in the U.S. Some appreciated the gift, but from most I never heard anything.

Finishing a Dream

Five years and many library copies later, I got the idea to put the book on Internet – the modern way to distribute information. There it would be available instantly to the entire world! It would also save me a lot of postage and trouble. So I began revising the book for the Internet because by now 14 years had passed since the original edition, and there was room for many additions and improvements. Still, much of the text stood the test of time, I believed, and the book could yet serve as an easily readable and practical introduction to living with fewer resources and less impact on the earth.

Just as I finished revising the book for Internet, and being a different person now, it occurred to me, wouldn't an international publisher be able to spread the book and its message even better? I decided to give it a try, and sent the manuscript to five likely publishers. One responded positively, Green Books in the U.K., the people who put out publications by E. F. Schumacher, one of my inspirers. I came to agreement with Green Books and rewrote the book with their editorial help to meet the British audience in the year 2004.

I was happy, but still not quite satisfied, because it was not readily available outside of Britain, and freight charges made it expensive.

So I decided to finish my idea of putting it up on Internet, to which Green Books generously agreed. A few weeks later it was up for free download at: http://www.alternativ.nu/ecologybeginsathome/.

This was kindly hosted by the Swedish web site for self-sufficiency, http://www.alternativ.nu

At Last: Peace, Joy and Satisfaction

Now, at last, I can relax, satisfied and peaceful. My work is done, my gift given. I have come to understand that what matters most in life is to give our gifts, whatever they are. If I hold back, I feel stingy and unfulfilled – out of nothing comes nothing. When I give, I create something where before there was nothing. I plant a seed that can grow into something and may some day give back – either to me or to someone else. I have learned that I must believe in myself and dare to do what feels right in my life, day by day, action by little action. Each time I do that, I experience the satisfaction it gives at the time, and then with its memory even in all the years to come. And like a seed, the gift may grow, providing ever more joy and satisfaction, as it did with my first letter titled Ecology Begins at Home and sent out to a hundred friends.

When a dream, big or small, arises in your mind, seize the opportunity. Believe in yourself, in your own uniqueness, in your own special way of doing things, with your own something special to give to the world. Publishing my book, and doing it myself, with my own hands at the Writer's Book Machine, has meant more to me than anything else I have done in life, except being a father and teaching. Were I to die tomorrow, my life would be complete – my book is out, my message said, my gift given. Let me encourage you to do the same!

You can be a good finisher

Let's return to the steps you can take as you get close to your picture of success. "When you have done 80% of the work, there is only 80% left," we are told. Bad maths, but it illuminates the effort involved in finishing. So how can you be a good finisher? Let's imagine that you are a long way down the road toward completing your 'project' – be it writing a book, leading a team, launching a product or whatever. The end is in sight, but the greatest task may lie ahead. As Joseph Campbell wrote: "There is often a final challenge before lifting the Grail." Be calm, controlled and centered. Be fully present. Love the process as much as the prize. Keep doing the right things and finishing will happen as a by-product – like an apple dropping from the tree. Let's explore how you can flow, focus and finish.

You can follow your successful style for finishing

Finishing is a key skill in life. "Keep working until you complete the job," sound simple in theory, but people can lose concentration, get side-tracked or fall at the final hurdle. So how does it work in practice? How can you complete a book, perform well to the final whistle in a sporting event or finish a project successfully? Here are three ideas worth considering.

Clarify your successful pattern for finishing

Try tackling the later exercise called *Finishing*. Looking back at your life, describe something you have finished successfully. What did you do right then? Be super specific. For example, one person said:

"Five years ago I finally completed work on refurbishing the 'Granny annexe' at our house, something I had delayed for years. First, I decided whether or not I wanted to do it. Certainly I could have hired a local builder – which would have freed up time – but I chose to finish it myself. Second, I set aside time to do the job, booking long weekends over a period of 12 months. I ring-fenced this time, rather than allowing it to become cluttered by other events. Third, I established a working ritual, starting on Friday morning, working all day and most of Saturday, then allocating the rest of the weekend to the family. Fourth, I made it as pleasurable as possible, playing my favourite music, listening to the radio and having frequent coffee breaks. Fifth, I followed the discipline and kept working until it was finished. Now my teenage kids have moved into that part of the house – so Granny will have to wait."

Clarify your successful pattern for finishing – then consider how you can follow similar principles in the future. (You may have different successful patterns in your personal and professional life. For example, when moving-on from a relationship or completing a work project.) Then go onto the next step.

Choose something you want to finish

Looking into the future, choose something you want to finish. Be selective to be effective. You can't complete everything in life. Providing you accept the consequences, it can be okay to say: "I don't want to finish it." Identify what you want to finish and treat it like a 'project'. Start by clarifying your picture of perfection. Recognise the pluses and minuses involved in reaching the goal – then decide whether you want to go for it. If so, clarify the three things you can do to give yourself the greatest chance of success. Create a road map – a project plan – for achieving the picture of perfection.

Create the time to tackle the project, follow your successful pattern and keep working until you finish

Set aside time to finish, otherwise you are destined to fail. Break down the task into reasonable chunks. Set yourself achievable goals for each time period so that you can get a sense of achievement. Follow your successful pattern and develop daily disciplines. Twyla Tharp, the choreographer, recommends establishing positive rituals. Now in the 60's, she starts her day at 5.30 am and walks out of her flat onto the Manhattan Street. She then hails a cab that takes her to the gym for a two-hour workout. Twyla believes that it is vital to start the day properly. Writing in her book *The Creative Habit*, she explains:

"Being creative is an everyday thing, a job with its own routines…The routine is as much part of the creative process as the lightening bolt of inspiration (perhaps more). And it is available to everyone. If creativity is a habit, then the best creativity is a result of good work habits."

Keep doing the right things – but also look ahead and rehearse potentially difficult scenarios. "Critical moments are the key," said one athlete. "The prize is almost within my grasp – sometimes I lift it, sometimes it slips away. How can I finish properly at those crucial moments?"

You can practice the art of mental rehearsal

Peak performers know it is important to relax and rehearse to get great results. "My best performances have come after preparing properly," said one person. "Failing to prepare results in catastrophe." Here are three tips for practicing mental rehearsal before entering a challenging situation.

Relax

Rest and relax. Get enough sleep – otherwise you may feel edgy. Different people relax in different ways. Some lie in the bath rehearsing the day ahead, some set aside quiet time to plan, some arrive an hour before a customer appointment and sit in the car park gathering their thoughts. Relax in the way that is right for you.

Rehearse

Re-centre and rehearse. Zen Masters re-centre by ensuring they feel fully present in the moment so they can give their full attention to a person or experience. Other people re-centre in other ways. One person said: "I start the day by focusing on my life goals. Starting from this destination, I clarify how what I will be doing that day will contribute to achieving this picture. Seeing the connection helps me to feel stronger and provides a sense of meaning."

Move on to the rehearsal. Looking ahead to the situation, clarify the real results you want to achieve. Anticipate all the possible scenarios. What is the best that can happen? How could you build on that success? What is the worst that can happen? How can you prevent that taking place? What can you do if it does happen? After considering the different scenarios, settle-on your chosen strategy. Practice what must be done to achieve the goals.

Results

Refocus on the picture of perfection. Relax – then prepare to step onto stage. Develop and individual ritual for snapping into 'alert mode' before entering the arena – be it the football field, customer presentation or whatever. Be fully present in the situation. Then do everything possible to deliver positive results.

You can become a class act

"They are a class act," is a phrase used to describe somebody who consistently performs brilliantly – and often adds that touch of class. The footballer scores with a breathtaking volley; the singer produces a memorable encore; the 'victor' behaves generously; the 'loser' makes a gracious speech; the soldier behaves courageously in the heat of battle. Such people demonstrate grace under pressure. Who do you think is a class act?

Nelson Mandela, for example, turned away from violence and personally thanked his warders when leaving Robbins Island. Lady Maria Stubbs set the tone when taking over the school where Philip Lawrence was murdered. On her first day at St Georges, Westminster, she shook hands with every pupil. Tackling the challenge head-on, she worked with the staff and students to turn around the school. Alison Fulford is brilliant at customer service. Faced by schisms between angry customers and the company, she is able to find 'win-win' solutions. How can you become a class act? Here are three suggestions you may want to consider.

Choose an activity in which you have the ability to become a class act

One football coach chose to become the outstanding head of a youth academy, rather than a highly paid club manager. "My skills are in helping talented young players to develop," he said. "They are not suited to the roller-coaster pressures of getting weekly results and talking with the press. I prefer to produce a succession of young players who go on to become internationals." Clarify the activity in which you stand a chance of becoming a class act.

Perform brilliant work to reach at least a 9/10 – then add that touch of class.

Be super professional. Do everything possible to deliver success. Sometimes you may achieve your goal by adding a touch of class. Different people show class in different ways. Sometimes they do 'something special'. Sometimes they find a solution that seems stunningly simple – but therein lies its magic. Looking back, can you think of a time when you added that 'touch of class'? Perhaps it was when you had already completed a task, then added that little bit extra; or during a 'critical' moment – when you performed well under pressure. What did you do right then to do something special? Try tackling the later exercise called *Becoming A Class Act*. Looking to the future, describe what you can do to add that touch of class.

When in doubt, ask yourself: "What would a class act do in this situation?" Then do it.

Sometimes you will hit problems that upset you personally. For example, you may suffer unfair personal criticism. Buy time and ask yourself: "What would a class act do in this situation?" Try the later exercise on this theme called *Class Act Thinking*. Looking ahead, think of an unsettling challenge. Consider what a great human being would do in this situation. Bearing this in mind, clarify how you can behave in that way – then do it. For example, be calm, kind and super creative. Maybe you won't always 'win'. But you will keep your dignity, be true to yourself and feel happier as a human being. That is the hallmark of a class act.

Katie Ledger helps people to take this step in high pressure situations. An outstanding communications coach, she believes that 'everybody has a unique story to tell'. People often freeze, however, when put in front of a camera, speaking into a microphone or giving a business speech. Katie helps them to relax, rehearse and be real – whether in front of a camera or meeting a staff member in the lift. Extremely professional, she does this by being caring yet also giving practical tools. She is much more than a 'media coach'. She helps people to clarify their messages, bring these to life and be themselves when communicating with different audiences. Katie's transition from news room to helping people tell their stories is described in the piece called *Making an Impact.*

Making an Impact: the journey of a professional story maker

Katie Ledger

I always feel everybody has a unique story to tell. The most powerful interviews I've conducted have not been with politicians or celebrities. They've been with people who have been passionate about a 'cause' – usually something greater than themselves.

That got me thinking about how I could help more people to tell their stories. Stories are an incredibly powerful way to get your key messages across and tell the audience a little about yourself. People respond warmly to someone who doesn't need to "stick to the script". They respect somebody who knows their subject and has a good sense of humour. In a complex world where audiences can only recall so much information, the memorable stories will serve as your calling card. Stories are also much easier for a speaker to remember – reducing the fear of forgetting what you want to say. This is my story.

Four years ago I had a vision. At the time I was a news presenter for ITN. I started 'moonlighting' by hosting a corporate conference and doing voice-over work on a corporate video. That made me realise I could transfer the strengths and the skills I learnt as a TV news presenter to make a real impact in the corporate world.

Getting started was relatively simple, but it still required quite a bit of work. Providing I did a good job, however, word of mouth brought other opportunities. This was fortunate because, 3 years after starting the corporate assignments, the TV channel I worked for changed its news provider. The moonlighting put me in a good position to be my own boss and hit the ground running. The challenge was expanding the previous part-time work into a sustainable business.

Step 1: Knowing strengths.

When interviewing people, I have always aimed to create an environment in which they could tell their stories. People say I've always been good at talking – though I also hope I am a good listener! The key is to help interviewees feel at ease enough to tell the story from their own perspective. This is something I have always enjoyed doing.

Twelve years of talking to camera on live TV also teaches you how to deal with stressful situations. The voice in your ear may be saying: "Keep talking for 30 seconds till we get the feed from the disaster." You must appear relaxed, even when perching on a stool, and 'talk to time'. You need to say something sensible to the viewers till you get the live feed. Then the real work starts as you try to work out, in real time, what is happening. It's a great learning experience. Almost nothing can beat live TV.

So how could I shape a career in the corporate world? TV had taught me lots of about presenting and editing, whilst I had also reported for local radio. Looking at the corporate world, I saw the possibilities to help speakers to bring their messages to life and help organisations engage with their audiences. Clarifying these strengths was the first step to developing the new business.

Step 2: Building on strengths

The next step was to know how to use these strengths in, what for me, was a relatively new world. How was it possible to use them to best effect in the corporate environment? I was fortunate enough to meet a business coach who helped me to shape my thinking around what I could offer to organisations.

'Media training' seemed the obvious label. But it's not something I get asked to do regularly. Instead, the approach I take helps people to feel comfortable sharing their stories with anybody through any medium. The first step is to help them to clarify their message. We then work on how they can be natural and present their story in a compelling way. It can be via a corporate video, blogging, presenting at conferences, round table discussions, meeting their boss or being interviewed by a journalist. The big challenge facing communicators, however, is that today's 'audiences" are very savvy. They can see whether or not a person actually 'believes' in their message. So it is important for communicators to be real. Your face and body have to be saying the same as your words.

Step 3: Positioning.

The challenging part was 'positioning' what I could offer to clients, but once we met face-to-face it was much easier. My starting point was always: "What are you working on now? What is your major challenge today? How can I help?" Frequently we returned to the same themes: "We want to communicate our vision in an exciting way…to really engage our people…to make keynote speeches more personal, rather than rely on PowerPoint."

Once we had established the goals, we clarified the messages and worked on finding real ways to bring these to life. During company conferences, for example, I often interviewed the boss in front of the employees. People seemed to appreciate it, because I asked the boss tough questions. Strangely, this often led to more work, even from the boss who I had given a tough time.

Step 4: Reaching out

Customers buy certainty. So the most effective promotional tool is word of mouth. People are more likely to buy something that has been recommended by somebody else in their network. I began reaching out by writing a basic biography with references and setting-up a website. Then I got help from people in my network. Several freelancers I knew worked with leaders in organisations. Our offerings were complementary, rather than competitive. So I asked if they would be willing to recommend me, providing they genuinely felt their client would benefit. I would, of course, recommend them to my clients. After getting a piece of work, the aim was to do a great job and add a touch of class that would make a personal impact. It was important to leave a lasting impression so that customers wanted to tell others. Fortunately this happened.

Step 5: Knowing your audience.

The target market I choose to work with are pacesetters – those who are at the leading edge. Such people and organisations are driven and prepared to give 100% to achieve their goals. They are not afraid to shake things up if necessary – whether that means re-designing a conference from scratch, answering tough questions or considering a new medium, such as corporate blogs. Doing live TV can be addictive – because of the adrenalin involved – and I still love working with people who are prepared to be adventurous.

Steps 1.5, 2.5, 3.5 and 4.5 recurring. Balancing!

The last few years have been exciting. But the real challenge has been sustaining satisfaction in both my personal and professional lives. It's the hardest balancing act to pull off, but the most fulfilling. I believe that to be truly happy it is important to harmonise these two areas of your life. For me, it's about organising myself around the demands of these two areas of my life and most importantly, continuously managing my energy and self-expectation. With all the varying demands of being a working mum, I often need to create the space and time to just think things through. The hardest lesson has been to learn that I can no longer just say "Yes, I'll do it. I'll be there in 5."

Moving Forward

Now I am moving into new areas. Today, I am fascinated by how people can use technology to improve their own and other people's lives. So I work for BBC TV's 'Click' and other programmes that spread this message around the world. In the 'old days' I spent most of my time in 'conventional' media. That was great – but it didn't reach the parts where some of our best stories are being lived. So I decided to explore deeper. That led me to work with some large high-tech companies and a better understanding of how technology can positively affect people's lives.

Today's online experience can bring people together like never before. Age, race, wealth, gender – there are very few barriers to entry. Social networking sites for business, students, gamers, people who do craft and also dogs (yes, dogs). Blogs carry such a wealth of commentary and stories on specific subjects. Instant Messenger and Skype also enable people to communicate free anywhere in the world! And it is all about people telling their stories.

Certainly it has been an interesting journey. But I couldn't achieve this without a great support team: my husband, my children and my mum (part-time nanny). I love being my own boss – not having to answer to anyone but it does take a lot of hard work and energy. I constantly remind myself of the saying: "You only get out what you put in." It's true.

You can flow, focus and finish

Let's return to your picture of success. Imagine you are embarking on the final phase of your chosen project. The way you finish will obviously depend on what you are doing – be it writing a book, building a house or whatever – but the principles remain similar. Flow, focus and finish. There are many different examples we could explore to highlight these themes, but let's consider just one.

Imagine that you will be giving a 40 minute keynote speech to a conference audience of 300 people. You have prepared properly and are ready to step on stage. During the weeks leading up to this moment:

- You have researched the audience and know the key challenges they face. You have a good idea what they want to 'take away' from the 40 minute session. You have pictured what you want the audience to be saying, thinking and feeling when they leave the auditorium.

- You know your 'script' and the 3 key messages you want to give to the audience. You know how to bring the speech to life with real examples. You know how to grab the audience and keep them engaged.

- You have broken-down the 40 minute speech into four 10 minutes sections so that you can pace yourself properly. You have rehearsed everything down to the last detail. You have practiced so that you can 'forget' and use your natural personality.

Calm, controlled and centered, you are ready to step on stage. Now all you need to do is to flow, focus and finish. Let's explore these steps.

Flow

Looking back, recall when you experienced a sense of flow in similar situations. Recall what you did right then – and how you can follow similar principles today. Be fully present in the moment. Take a deep breath and step onto the stage. Welcome the audience and move into your first '10 minute' slot. Speak calmly and establish credibility. Connect with your audience's aspirations. Explain the 'take aways' they will get from the session. Give your first key message. Bring it to life with real examples that resonate with your audience. Relax and flow.

Focus

Be 100% engaged. Put your soul into your presentation. Be yourself. Use your body, voice and different media to bring your messages to life. Then embrace the paradox. Give everything to the present moment, but focus on your end goal – the picture of perfection. Picture again what you want people saying when they leave the auditorium. Complete the first '10 minute slot' – then make a bridge to the second 10 minutes. Give your second key message – and practical tools that people can use to achieve success. Change the tempo. Vary your voice; vary the examples; vary the media. Move onto the third '10 minute' slot. People think they know what is coming, so do something surprising. Move into the final 10 minutes. You are now running around the final curve.

Finish

Pause before your final effort. Give a great example that people will remember – a story they will recognise from their personal or professional life. Repeat your 3 key messages. Describe the practical steps people can take to get an early success. Change the tempo in the last minute. Thank people for their time and wish them luck for the rest of the conference. The tape is now in sight. Get ready for your final 'party piece'. Relax – then launch into the final 30 seconds. Flow, focus and finish – with a bang!

Conclusion

The Strengths Way is a positive way of working with people. Everybody is an artist, everybody is creative. Everybody can build on their strengths and give something special to the world. There are many models for understanding the stages people go through in their lives. Here is one that is based on the Five Seasons of Life. Spring, Summer, Autumn, Winter and then your Second Spring.

Childhood is your first spring. The fields are green, the sky is blue and you can wander forever. Providing you are given encouragement, every day is an adventure. You can discover the world, discover your talents and follow your dreams. Summer is a time for sitting in cafes and discussing how to change the world. Teenage years throb with idealism. Providing you receive guidance, you discover your vocation and travel the road of giving what you can to the world.

Autumn is the time when you begin worrying about 'security'. Perhaps idealism doesn't work after all; perhaps you had better get a 'proper job'. You look for a partner, forget your life passion and begin saving for a life-pension. You get a mortgage, work hard and try to establish security. Providing you hit the company targets, you gain promotion and climb the corporate ladder – perhaps gathering more debts.

Winter arrives one day. Sitting in a traffic jam, you say: "I am successful, but I am not happy. What do I really want out of life? How can I do it straight away?" Failing to see an immediate answer, you numb yourself and gain another promotion. One day another wake-up call arrives. You hear about a school friend who has died. They were the same age as you. So you embark on the existential journey travelled by people over the years: "Who am I? What do I want to do? Why do I want to it? How can I do it? And when?"

You may stay in your job, but begin pursuing a parallel strategy. People develop – they don't change. "Be who you are, only more so," is the message. You learn how to channel your personality, rather than change your personality. Accepting your talents, you look for the right balance between money, meaning and magic. Money feeds the stomach, but meaning and magic feed the spirit and the soul. You say 'Yes,' to spending time with positive people – but 'No,' to negative people. Winter is tough, but it can also be beautiful. Here comes the sun.

Then comes your Second Spring. Choosing to live life, you embrace Neil Young's words: "It is better to burn out, than it is to rust." You want to live the vital life, rather than the vanilla life. There is nothing more delightfully dangerous than a person in their second spring. You recapture your zest and feel alive. You do what you want, dress the way you want and spend time with the people you want. You learn to balance your soul work and salary work, mission and mortgage, fulfilment and finances. Life is for living and you enjoy every day. That doesn't mean everything is rosy.

Sometimes you go through all five seasons in one day. But now you have perspective. You have stronger control needs but, paradoxically, accept some things you can't control. You do good work in your 'Garden', whilst contributing toward building a better Globe. You are here to serve. So it is time to plant more seeds of hope in your Second Spring. You may not see them blossom, but that doesn't matter. Sometimes your flowers will grow tomorrow.

People want to follow their dreams – and they have often done so by following the peak performer's path. They follow their passion and translate it into a clear purpose. Super professional, they find solutions to problems, achieve peak performance and pass on their knowledge. Sometimes they enjoy a sense of peace. Take the ideas you like from this book and plant seeds in your own way. Enjoy the journey.

Success:

Trigger Questions

The following pages provide trigger questions that a person can use to perform superb work, find solutions, help others and work towards achieving success.

a) Superb Work

- What are the key strategies you must follow to give yourself the greatest chance of success? How can you keep following these strategies in your daily work?

- How can you make sure you are following your road map towards achieving the picture of perfection? How can you keep checking your 'compass'? How can you build-in time for 'course correction'?

- How can you follow your daily disciplines? How can you make good use of your 'prime times'?

- How can you be super professional in your work? How can you give superb service to customers? If you have sponsors to satisfy, how you can reassure them by getting some early wins?

- How can you stay proactive? How can you keep tackling issues that are in the green, amber and red zones?

b) Solutions

- Looking ahead, what are the potential difficulties you may face? How can you anticipate and prevent these difficulties happening? How can you manage them if they do happen?

- How can you find creative solutions to challenges? If appropriate, how can you use the Five C Model for problem-solving? How can you focus on the challenges, choices, consequences, creative solutions and conclusions?

- How can you overcome setbacks? How can you take yourself through the reactive change curve? How give you give yourself time in a sanctuary, start shaping your future then achieve success?

- How can you get support? How can you start out by making clear contracts about the support you need to do the job? How can you support yourself?

- How can you spend time with your encouragers – the 'pot fillers'? How can you manage your stoppers – the 'pot drillers'?

- How can you encourage yourself? How can you record your achievements? How can you clarify what you are doing right each day? How can you remind yourself to count your blessings?

- How can you build in time for rest and recovery? How can you make good use of the fallow times? How can you build in time for 'slow thinking'?

c) Service

- How can you use your strengths to help others to succeed? When are you best at giving? How can you put yourself in more situations and give your best to people?

- How can you be a good encourager? How can you help people by focusing on encouragement, enterprise and excellence?

- How can you pass on your professional and personal knowledge? Imagine you were invited to give 3 key messages to a group of 18-year-olds about things they might bear in mind in their future lives. What would be the 3 key messages you would give to them? How can you encourage future generations?

d) Success

- How can you be a good finisher? What is your successful style for finishing? Looking back at your past, what have you finished successfully? What did you do right then? How can you follow these principles in the future? How can you give yourself the time and chance to finish?

- How can you satisfy your sponsors? How can you fulfil your contracts and deliver on your promises? How can you do everything possible to reach your goals? How can you double-check that your sponsors are happy?

- How can you become a Class Act? Looking at your past, can you recall a time when – even if only for a moment – you behaved like a Class Act? What did you do right then? How can your follow similar principles in the future? What are the activities you can pursue in which you have a chance to become a class act? What must you do to get to at least 9/10? How can you then add that touch of class?

- How can you finish? Looking ahead to challenges, how can you relax and rehearse to get results? How can you flow, focus and finish?

- Looking to the future, how can you find the next satisfying project? How can you continue to use your strengths to help other people? How can you help to build a positive planet?

Success

Exercises

The following pages provide exercises that a
person can use to work towards achieving success

Professionalism:
The Do's & Don't's

**Do's. The specific things I must do to
be super professional in my work are:**

- ....
- ....
- ....
- ....
- ....
- ....
- ....

**Don't's. The specific things I must not do if I
am to be super professional in my work are:**

- ....
- ....
- ....

Daily Disciplines

The specific things I must do in the right way every day to get the right results are to:

- ....

  ....

- ....

  ....

- ....

  ....

- ....

  ....

- ....

  ....

Staying Proactive: The Green, Amber & Red Zones

The Green Zone.
The things that are going well are:

● ....

The steps I can take to build on these things are:

● ....

The Amber Zone.
The things that are going okay but there may be warning signs are:

● ....

The steps I can take to build on these things are:

● ....

The Red Zone.
The things that are going badly or where I experience real pressure are:

● ....

The steps I can take to build on these things are:

● ....

Managing Setbacks Successfully

**A time in my life when I managed
a setback successfully was when I:**

● ....

**The specific things I did right then to
overcome the setback successfully were:**

● ....

● ....

● ....

● ....

● ....

**Bearing these lessons in mind, the specific things
I can do to manage setbacks in the future are:**

● ....

● ....

● ....

The Five C Creative Problem-Solving Framework

The challenge I want to tackle is:

● *How to*..

Step 1: Challenge
Looking at the challenge, the
***Real Results* I want to achieve are:**

a) To...

b) To...

c) To...

Step 2: Choices

The possible options for tackling this challenge are:

a) To...

b) To...

c) To...

<u>Step 3: Consequences</u>

OPTION A: To...

      Pluses   *Minuses*

- ....   • ....

- ....   • ....

      Attractiveness Rating:............................/10

OPTION A: To...

      Pluses   *Minuses*

- ....   • ....

- ....   • ....

      Attractiveness Rating:............................/10

OPTION A: To...

      Pluses   *Minuses*

- ....   • ....

- ....   • ....

      Attractiveness Rating:............................/10

<u>Step 4: Creative Solutions</u>

The possible creative solutions are:

- To..

- To..

- To..

<u>Step 5: Conclusions</u>

The chosen option – or options – I want to pursue are:

- To..

- To..

- To..

The specific steps I can therefore take to deliver concrete results are:

- To..

- To..

- To..

My Self-Confidence Pot

Pot Fillers
**The people who put encouragement
and energy into my pot are:**

- ....
- ....

- ....
- ....

- ....
- ....

**The things I do to put encouragement
and energy into my pot are:**

- ....
- ....

- ....
- ....

- ....
- ....

Pot Drillers
**The people who discourage
or take away energy are:**

- ....
- ....

- ....
- ....

- ....
- ....

The things I do to discourage myself or take away energy are:

- ....
- ....
- ....

- ....
- ....
- ....

<u>My Action Plan</u>
The specific things I can do to put encouragement and energy into my pot are:

- ....
- ....
- ....

The specific things I can do to fill the holes in my pot are:

- ....
- ....
- ....

My Right Book

Three things I did right today were:

- ....

- ....

- ....

**The things I can do to follow
these principles in the future are:**

- ....

- ....

- ....

**Two things I can do even better
in the future – and how – are:**

- ....

- ....

My Assets

The personal & professional
assets that I have are:

- ....

- ....

- ....

- ....

- ....

- ....

- ....

- ....

- ....

Results Require Rest & Recovery

**The specific things I can do to rest
and recover properly in the future are:**

- ....

....

- ....

....

- ....

....

The benefits of doing these things will be:

- ....

....

- ....

....

- ....

....

The Fallow Times

The specific things I can do to give myself permission to be fallow are to:

- ....

- ....

- ....

The specific things I can do to make good use of the fallow times are to:

- ....

- ....

- ....

The specific things I can do to take the right opportunity to then move back into flow are to:

- ....

- ....

- ....

Slow Thinking

**The situations in which I can
do some slow thinking are:**

- ....

....

- ....

....

- ....

....

**The steps I can take to give myself more
opportunities for slow thinking are to:**

- ....

....

- ....

....

- ....

....

My Sanctuaries

My sanctuaries are:

- ....

- ....

- ....

The benefits of spending time

in these sanctuaries are:

- ....

- ....

- ....

The steps I can to take to make good

use of these sanctuaries are to:

- ....

- ....

- ....

The Art of Giving

The situations where I am good at giving are:

● ....

The things I do right to give then are:

● ....

● ....

● ....

The things I can do to keep giving are to:

● ....

● ....

● ....

The Art of Encouragement

**Looking back on my life, some
of my key encouragers have been:
The person's name (1):**

- ....

The specific things they did to encourage me were:

- ....

- ....

- ....

The person's name (2):

- ....

The specific things they did to encourage me were:

- ....

- ....

- ....

The person's name (3):

- ....

The specific things they did to encourage me were:

- ....

- ....

- ....

Bearing in mind these – and other – principles, the key things I want to do to encourage people are to:

- ....

- ....

- ....

Finishing

**A time I finished something
successfully was when I:**

- ....

**The specific things I did to
finish successfully then were:**

- ....

- ....

- ....

**The specific things I can do to finish
things successfully in the future are to:**

- ....

- ....

- ....

Passing on Knowledge

Professional Knowledge
**The professional knowledge that I can
Pass on to people is in the following areas:**

● How to..

**The things I can to do pass on
this knowledge to people are:**

● ....

Personal Knowledge
**The personal knowledge that I can
pass on to people is in the following areas:**

● *How to...*

**The things I can to do pass on
this knowledge to people are to:**

● ....

Wise Words

Imagine you have been invited to give 3 messages to a group of 18-year-old about the things to bear in mind during their lives. Describe the messages you would give and bring these to life with examples.

The 3 messages I would give
the young people would be:

1) ....

For example:

....

2) ....

For example:

....

3) ....

For example:

....

Becoming a Class Act

**The specific activity in which I want to become
– and feel I can become – a class act is:**

- ....

- ....

- ....

**The specific things I must do to deliver superb
work – and reach at least a 9/10 – in this activity
are:**

- ....

- ....

- ....

**The specific things I can then do
to add that *touch of class* are to:**

- ....

- ....

Class Act Thinking. "What Would a Class Act Do In This Situation?"

**The potentially difficult situation
I could face in the future could be:**

- ....

**The things a class act would
do in this situation would be:**

- ....

- ....

- ....

**The things I can do to behave like
a class act in this situation are to:**

- ....

- ....

- ....

The Flowing Life

**The specific situation in which I want
to flow, focus, finish in the future is:**

•
....

....

....

**The specific things I can do to flow,
focus and finish in this situation are to:**

•
....

•
....

•
....

The Second Spring

The things I want to do in my second spring are to:

- ....

- ....

- ....

The steps I can take to do some of these things now are:

- ....

- ....

- ....